CULTS
How They Work.

CULTS – How They Work

First published in 2008

ISBN 978-0-620-42357-1

Cults: How They Work
Jacko Consulting
P.O.Box 16079
Bluff
4036
Durban
South Africa

CULTS
How They Work.

By
Robin Jackson

JACKO CONSULTING

It is good to learn what to avoid by studying the misfortunes of others.-

Publius Syrius

Author's Preface

We live in a society where people are free to follow and adhere to the religious belief of their choice. I have no quarrel with this. It is possible to disagree with a person's beliefs and yet love the person holding those beliefs. What I oppose are some of the teachings and overbearing influence of some of these groups, not the people in the groups or their right to believe whatever they want.

I also acknowledge that many of the founders of some of these groups do not deceive their followers intentionally. Some of them may have begun a sincere search for truth, but ended up with a warped sense of reality and truth. Likewise, the followers of many of these cults also set out on their journeys to search for truth, but fell captive to unscrupulous deceivers out to fleece and control them. Case in point is the statement allegedly made by the founder of the Church of Scientology, Lafayette Ron Hubbard, who spoke before a science fiction writer's convention and said, *"Writing for a penny a word is ridiculous. If a man really wanted to make a million dollars, the best way would be to start his own religion."*

Furthermore, labelling a certain group a cult can be controversial and some people may disagree with me in labelling some groups as such. This in part is due to the fact that some of these groups have received mainstream religious status because of the immense number of followers they command. Others prefer to label these as *high control groups* or *new religious movements*. However, I do not differentiate between these terms in this book because the mode of operation of these groups, regardless of what you may call them, is similar. Therefore, I label them all cults.

As a former cult member, I have witnessed first hand the inner workings of these groups and how similar their methods of recruitment and control are. My first book, *Losing The Faith: Truth under Scrutiny* is the account of my journey through one of the largest cults in the world today, namely, the Jehovah's Witnesses. Since the publication of that very same book the consequences that I, as well as my immediate family, have experienced only reiterates how destructive cults can be. Loss of friends and family are just two of the results that members who eventually leave a cult must face and endure. Many come to the realization that love and friendships in cults are conditional. In addition, some cults are just plain deadly.

My desire is for this work to serve as a reference and a guide; one that will assist people to recognise the dangers and pitfalls of becoming involved with cults. An appendix is provided at the end of this book from which readers can explore the writings and research of former cult members. This book is not intended to promote or endorse a particular religion or belief structure.

Acknowledgements

I am deeply indebted and grateful to a long list of people whom I have never met. This includes those whom I have corresponded with via e-mail, telephone calls and normal snail mail. Those who have published their personal accounts of their times in cults as well as the consequences they have suffered for standing up for truth I greatly admire. You are too numerous to mention.

To my sisters, Ronelle Brink and Penny Cloete, thank you for your encouragement and continued support.

To Nick Georgiades, who so generously supplied me with information on Freemasonry and loaned me literature for my research into secret societies. Thank you very much. I am greatly indebted to you.

To Bruce and Beverley Biggar, thank you for your support and friendship.

CULTS – How They Work

Robin Jackson

Contents

9

Introduction

The morning of March 26 1997 started just like any other day in San Diego, United States. However, by the end of that day America saw the biggest mass suicide in its history. Thirty-nine members of a religious cult called Heaven's Gate, fed themselves a lethal cocktail of Phenobarbital, apple sauce and vodka in an attempt to reach for the stars. Before this tragic incident almost no one had heard of the cult and understandably there was now a hunger for information that would shed some light on the bewildering actions of the group. The world soon learnt that members were polite, quiet, and made a living designing Web pages for commercial clients. On the outside they seemed like normal people, who were well groomed and who got on very well with their neighbours. If only their own website was scrutinised, we would have seen that it was there that they started announcing their sinister beliefs and ultimate intentions.

Heaven's Gate announced that they were aliens sent to earth for a brief period and that soon a UFO would come and take them away. That UFO was supposedly concealed in the tail of the comet Hale-Bopp. Faithfully by night the group scanned the skies by means of their telescopes, yearning for the moment when they would leave this sinful world behind. That moment arrived and the group announced the news on-line: 'Our joy is that our Older Member has made it clear to us that Hale-Bopp's approach is the marker we've been waiting for. We are happily prepared to leave this world.' Prepared in more ways than one they definitely were, for when their bodies were found in Rancho Santa Fe, the groups san Diego villa, they were neatly laid out on mattresses and bunks draped in purple ceremonial cloaks. Standing beside them were suitcases packed with personal belongings.

Through the ages man has seen its fair share of doomsday proclaimers. From Sybil in 195 to modern-day suicide cults, we have been preoccupied with proclaiming, speculating, and at times trying to hasten the end of this world. Here we only have to recall what happened at Waco, Texas where the Branch Davidians, under the cult leadership of David Koresh fought against the US military, believing it to be the start of their version of Armageddon.

Behind the perimeter fence of the Mount Carmel compound, and shielded from the prying eyes of the government, Koresh put his followers through intense Bible study classes. But that was not all, for he coupled the Bible study with equally intensive paramilitary training which included repeated screenings of the Vietnam War movies, Platoon and Full Metal Jacket. He also stockpiled an enormous amount of assault rifles, grenade launchers and machine guns. Koresh had successfully persuaded followers with his bizarre mixture of scriptural right with military might. This had been in place since the late eighties when he managed to persuade himself and his followers that he was the seventh angel of Revelation that has come to announce the Kingdom of God and to prepare them for the battle of Armageddon. When the authorities eventually caught up with him he had amassed $200,000 worth of ammunition and weapons. 'We're ready for war', he said.

When armed agents from the United States Bureau of Alcohol, Tobacco and Firearms arrived on 28 February 1993 to deliver a search warrant for illegal weapons, which they bungled up, six Branch Davidians and four agents were killed.

A stand-off that lasted fifty-one days ensued during which a FBI Hostage Rescue Team joined the BATF in an attempt to secure the surrender of Koresh and his followers. David Koresh was expecting the federal agents, not because he was sitting on a large stockpile of illegal weapons, but because they fell directly into his prophetic responsibility. He taught his followers that the Antichrist was at large in the world and its sole aim was to destroy the Davidians, God's elect, by using the American state as its unwitting instrument. Therefore, the FBI was an agent of Satan destined to meet their doom at Armageddon. So the showdown with the FBI was precisely what they were looking for. Furthermore, I strongly suspect they would have appreciated angelic assistance.

The aftermath of that standoff is forever etched in the minds of millions of television viewers around the world. The Waco compound exploded into flames and it became a tragedy from which only 9 out of 96 members walked out alive. However, many impartial commentators have admitted that the FBI could have handled the whole situation better.

Millions of members, who once thought they were immune to cult involvement, still do not know they are in one. Groups ranging from the Heaven's Gate cult on a small scale, to bigger groups such as the Jehovah's Witnesses, the Mormons, Church of Scientology and The Unification Church (Moonies) have all racked up immense numbers of followers. This only serves to reiterate how manipulative and deceptive cults can be. What makes these groups tick and win over so many followers? Why do people get involved in these dangerous cults? Think you are immune to being recruited into a cult? Think again!

Cults use sophisticated recruitment techniques to lure unsuspecting individuals to become members of their group. However, once recruited, the individuals are controlled by equally sophisticated mind control techniques that have been refined over time. Every aspect of the cult member's life is controlled by every utterance and teaching of the cult leadership. These leaders are often after your obedience, time and money.

To identify a cult we need to know how they work and understand the techniques used by these groups to win over individuals. I was once a member of one of the largest cults in the world today. Fortunately I got out, but of cause not without consequence.

This book exposes some of the secret techniques used by cults to mislead and control you. Once you understand these techniques you will be better equipped to spot and avoid cult recruiters and protect your family and friends. But be warned. This book contains information that cults do not want you to acquire.

Chapter 1

What is a Cult?

Where all think alike no-one thinks very much
Walter Lipman

CULTS – How They Work

The widely accepted definition of a "cult" is a group of individuals who share a set of religious or quasi-religious beliefs, often imposed by a charismatic leader or leaders, which tend not to conform to society's norm, and may be considered fanatical. Another definition is any group who uses mind control and deceptive recruitment techniques to trick people into joining, and thereafter to stay. However, many groups who fit this definition now prefer to be classified under the less contentious title of "new religious movement". The reason is because over the last fifty years the word "cult" has become synonymous with brainwashing, mass suicide, and even murder.

Their strong beliefs have originated mostly from dissatisfaction with mainstream religions. Moreover, influences of Christianity, Hinduism and Buddhism can be seen in many of today's cults. Therefore most of these cults cannot claim to be original, no-matter how off beat they may seem. Many imitate in one way or another older models. Confidently predicting the end of the world on such and such a date is merely reiterating a time honoured cliché.

A cult need not be a destructive group, despite popular preconceptions. Furthermore, many organizations that started out as cults have now become mainstream religions. In the United States, for example, Mormonism (Church of the Latter-day Saints of Jesus Christ) is nowadays seen as a respectable and genuine religious movement with its members actively recruited by the FBI and other government organizations. At the time of writing they even have a candidate running for President of the United States. However, the group did originate as a cult (and according to my observation still fit the profile) and some of their beliefs are anything but mainstream.

A lot depends on the qualities of the charismatic leader (or leaders). Just as a dictatorial political leader can be potentially dangerous, so too a dictatorial cult leader can be dangerous or even more so. Destructive cults are not only dangerous to their individual members, but to society as a whole. At the one end of the scale we have the most extreme of cults like the Japanese Aum Supreme Truth, which masterminded the nerve gas attacks on the Tokyo subway. On the other end, we have cults like the Moonies which will also have repercussions in wider society, even if it just means severing family ties.

This brings us to the different types of cults. The average person will be surprised to here that cults other than the religious types exist. The preconception is that cults are linked to religious fanaticism, but this is only partly true. They are classed into four types.

† Religious

Cults that use a religious belief system as their base are the most common type. This is the type that most of us are familiar with and that almost daily make the headlines around the world. Their basic belief system could be standard Christianity,

18

Islam, Hinduism or Buddhism. Some may even invent their own belief system. However, what makes them a cult is their use of mind control and not their beliefs.

† Counselling and Self-Help

Business people and big corporations are often targeted by cults using self-help and counselling as their base. By doing their courses they claim that you and your staff will become more successful. Business people are locked away in hotel rooms and are subjected to quasi-religious indoctrination while they play strange games and share their innermost thoughts with the group. As soon as you have completed the course you are told that you need to complete the more advanced one. This, of course, will cost you more money.

They often ask you to do volunteer work and to recruit family, friends and other workmates. They also specialise in creating very emotional experiences which are used to validate your involvement in the cult. The religious overtones are often hidden by using terms that do not sound religious. However, they usually surface towards the end of the seminar. Bankruptcy has often befallen many who have been involved in this type of cult.

† Commercial

"Cults of greed" are often what these types of cults are called. They use commercial gain as their base. Exceptional wealth is promised if you join the cult and follow their special programme. They often hold up their leader as an example and explain that by following the programme you will be just as successful. By using mind control these commercial cults get you to work for them for free and make you part with your cash to buy an endless stream of self-help books, tapes and seminars supposedly designed to help you succeed. In reality they are designed to enhance the cult's mind control environment and to keep you believing in their almost impossible dream of success.

Oh, and by the way, they never tell you that the primary way the leaders make their money is by selling those motivational materials that you buy! More about this in a later chapter.

† *Political*

History is littered with cults that use political ideals as their base. Classic examples of this type of cult are Hitler's Nazi Germany and Stalin's Communist USSR. This was mind control on a large scale. Here I am poised to include Apartheid South Africa albeit disagreement from some. On a smaller scale, white and black supremacists, terrorists, and rebel groups commonly use forms of mind control to recruit and dominate members. Under this type of cult we include examples such as The Michigan Militia, Posse Comitatus, The Nation of Islam and The Ku Klux Klan. And dare I include South Africa's very own AWB (Afrikaner Weerstand Beweeging).

†*Cargo Cults*

In the wake of interaction with technologically advanced non-native cultures, religious movements spring up in tribal societies. During the early part of the nineteenth century and following the Second World War, interaction between islanders and white immigrants was a shock to the natives. The natives were often fascinated by the wondrous possessions these white visitors to their shores had with them. What was even more fascinating was that when these things needed to be repaired they were sent away and new ones kept arriving as 'cargo' in ships or planes. The natives then concluded that this 'cargo' must be of a supernatural origin. The result is that the natives now devised ritual ceremonies which mimicked the actions of the white men colonizing the islands. David Attenborough in his book *Quest in Paradise* states:

> They build tall masts with wires attached to them; they sit listening to small boxes that glow with light and emit curious noises and strangled voices; they persuade the local people to dress in identical clothes, and march them up and down – and it would hardly be possible to devise a more useless occupation than that. And then the native realises that he has stumbled on the answer to the mystery. It is these incomprehensible actions that are the rituals employed by the white man to persuade the gods to send the cargo. If the native wants the cargo, then he too must do these things.

Locations such as New Guinea and other Micronesian and Melanesian countries in the southwest Pacific Ocean are locations where these religious movements became documented after initial contacts following exploration, colonization, missionary efforts, and international warfare.

The movie, *The Gods Must Be Crazy*, tells the fictional story of how a Coca-Cola bottle becomes accepted as a 'gift from the gods' after being discarded from a passing plane. The bottle subsequently falls on a native southwest African's head and is taken to the clan. Firstly it becomes revered as an object of prosperity which enhances the tribe's lives. However, after infighting breaks out the object is rejected. This presents a counter-example to cargo cults.

The cargo cults of the South Pacific do give us a fascinating glimpse as to how religions can spring up out of almost nothing.

† *Secret Societies*

The term "secret society" is one that is often misused and misunderstood. Many argue that you cannot call a certain organization a secret society if its existence is known. This definition is inaccurate. The fact that their inner workings are unknown to outsiders is what makes them secret. These secrets are protected by initiation ceremonies which impose penalties on those who betray them. Usually there is some ritualistic element to secret societies and therefore applying the term to Freemasonry, the Italian Carbonari or the Chinese Triads is justifiable. The two latter organizations might be seen as being more sinister but their rituals have much in common with the Freemasons. This, however, should come as no surprise.

The oldest secret society in the world, the Freemasons, has especially been thrust into the limelight in recent years. Books such as The Da Vinci Code and movies like National Treasure have thrown this sinister organization into the spotlight. Freemasons have been accused of everything from conducting underground satanic rituals to masterminding a worldwide conspiracy for planetary domination. The orders members – which have included Sir Isaac Newton, John Wayne, Bill Gates, some of the world's most popular entertainers, and twenty-five U.S. presidents – insist they merely share a bond of brotherhood, service, and charity.

It is estimated that some four to five million Freemasons worldwide pledge to live their lives in accordance with principles of morality, charity, and loyalty – both to fellow Masons and to the order itself. They engage in rituals and rites that is said to date back to the building of Solomon's Temple and the murder of its chief architect, Harim Abiff. However, Masons themselves differ in their view of the origins of Freemasonry with some claiming its origins to be in Egypt.

A friend of mine, Nick Georgiades, related his families experience when his father became a Freemason at the age of 18. Nick fondly remembers his father as an intelligent and charismatic man. Often he caught glimpses of his father practising Freemason rituals at home which encompassed secret handshakes and other elaborate displays. However, his father's membership of The Craft (as Freemasonry is called among its members) took a toll on his family's relationships. His father became non-existent to the family. "Our father was not a father to us, he was a father to the Freemasons," was the sentiment Nick expressed. Still today his mother views the Freemasons with much disdain.

Elements of Freemasonry can also be seen in many of today's cults. Joseph Smith was a Freemason and many of the Mormon temple rituals have much in common with Freemason rituals. Charles Taze Russell (Founder of The International Bible Students and later to become known as Jehovah's Witnesses) likewise used elements of Freemasonry in his early publications. The winged sun disk, a symbol of the Freemasons, can be seen on the covers of many of the books written by Russell. The cross and the crown surrounded by a wreath - another Mason symbol - used to appear on the covers of the early Watchtower magazines. Russell was also buried beneath a pyramid inscribed with the cross and crown emblem of the Freemasons.

Stephen Knight in his book, *The Brotherhood*, states that the Freemasons have a policy of mutual preferment. They help each other into jobs or contracts and out of jail. The book goes on to state they are popular in the police force and the judiciary. It seems as if Nick's mother is not the only disgruntled mother and widow of a Freemason. In 1989 Martin Short published his book *Inside The Brotherhood: Further Secrets of the Freemasons,* which mixed testimony from disgruntled Masonic widows and divorcees with claims that the Conservative Party in the UK was "riddled" with Freemasons.

Alright, for all intensive purposes and before the label "conspiracy theorist" gets added to my already well known "apostate" label, I will stop right there with the Freemasons. (I wouldn't want them also knocking on my door you know!)

Many books have been written about Freemasonry, both by members and non-members.

So, cults deceive people into joining and coerce them into staying. This is the definition that most people will agree with. Except for the cults of course. Now let's clear up some misconceptions about cults.

Chapter 2

Misconceptions about Cults

"Obvious thinking commonly leads to wrong judgements and wrong conclusions"

Humphrey B.Neil

The first preconceived image and misconception that most people have of cults is that they are easy to spot, wear weird clothes and live in communes. This of course is only partly true as some do fit this notion. For the most part cult members are everyday people like you and I. They live in houses, eat the same food and dress like the rest of us. The fact is that cult leaders do not want you to know that you are being recruited into a cult. The cult leaders therefore order their recruiters to dress in a way that will put you at ease. "Being relatable" is what one cult calls this technique.

The second misconception is that cults are full of weird, weak and emotionally unstable people. This is not true. Many intelligent, attractive and skilful people are members of a cult. Celebrities such as Tom Cruise, John Travolta, Elizabeth Taylor and Madonna have all become involved with cults. (However, after Tom Cruise's couch jumping interview on the Oprah Show I have doubts about the intelligent part.) Some have even been used to promote some of these controversial groups and to defend them. The very reason they are used by these groups is because of the public adulation and respect they enjoy. They are also often seen as role models and trendsetters.

In reality all sorts of people are involved with cults. One of the few common threads is that these people were often recruited at a low point in their lives. Most cults offer an escape-route to salvation; a special "nod from God" as it were, handed out to their devotees, which orthodox faiths, or so it is claimed, fails to supply. They are the sane ones while the rest of us are the lunatics destined to be destroyed.

The third misconception is that cults are just a bunch of religious nut cases. It is a common mistake people make. As we have seen in the previous chapter a cult refers to any group that uses mind control and devious recruitment techniques. The belief system of the cult often becomes warped to become a container for these techniques. We live in a free society and people are free to believe what they want. However, most would agree that it is wrong for anyone to deceive and control other people.

The fourth misconception is that Christians call all other groups cults. What this means is that if a group claims to be Christian and yet teaches something fundamentally different from the Bible, that group is classified as a cult. This book does not use this definition at all, but rather concentrates on the similarities across a broad spectrum of cults, whether their fundamental belief system be Christian, Jewish, Islamic, or whatever else. As I have said before, I intend to expose the common techniques used by all and what identifies them as such.

The American writer and journalist, Tom Wolfe, wrote that a cult is a religion with no political power. He definitely misunderstood the nature of that organism, for in reality, little could be further from the truth. Cults wield considerable power. Eight hundred years ago the entire political stability of southern France was threatened by the Catharists. Theirs was not an isolated phenomenon from history. Fast forward to modern 21st century Japan and the Soka Gakkai cult command a worldwide membership of over ten million. The largest of one hundred and eighty thousand registered sects in a country that lost its national religious identity at the end of World War II when its emperor, believed by many to be a living god, was forced to announce and admit defeat over the radio.

The Unification Church (Moonies) owns a multi-billion dollar business empire in America and openly voices global ambitions. The Watchtower organization (Jehovah's Witnesses), which has their headquarters in Brooklyn, New York, boasts a membership of more than six million worldwide and is a billion dollar corporation. And as mentioned before, the Mormons have a presidential candidate and a membership of more than ten million worldwide.

While it can be said that some cults hold views outside of the norms of society, they don't necessarily pose a threat to members of the wider community. Cults such as the modern Druids do follow leaders and hold special ceremonies and rituals, but they work to improve the environment for everybody, and membership doesn't involve rejecting society's entire value system. Many of the misconceptions may also stem from the fact that most of these cult practises are shrouded in secrecy. This has often led to media campaigns warning of supposed dangers.

Our impressions of the activities of secretive societies from our past are often coloured by romanticism and an idealised view of history, but many had sinister beginnings, and still have influence today. Moreover, it is important to maintain a balance between paranoid conspiracy theories, which sees a world that is dominated to this day by corrupt and powerful groups such as the Illuminati and the Freemasons, and a naïve refusal to believe that cults have ever wielded great influence.

No wonder that secretive organizations which believe they hold the key to a "new world order", or have the solutions to the problems of mankind, have been treated with suspicion.

The question that now arises is; "Doesn't our constitution protect the rights of these groups?" True, the constitution of South Africa and other countries does protect the rights of these groups in the areas of freedom of religion and speech. However, it is not a blanket protection for any actions done in the name of their beliefs. If a group breaks the law they are accountable for their actions just like everyone else. The constitution is not a suicide pact.

What many of these groups have forgotten is that the constitution is expansive and covers both their freedom and the freedom of speech of their critics.

Africa has seen its fair share of cult activity, not only from cults crossing over from America and Europe but from individual cults emerging on its own soil. Possibly the most deaths caused by a single cult that emerged from Africa are the deaths caused by *The Movement for the Restoration of the Ten Commandments*, a cult that emerged in Uganda. Just after the turn of the century, 780 bodies were found in a mass grave after a reign of terror that may have included murder and possibly mass suicide. However, due to the group operating in isolation many believe all the bodies will never be recovered and the death toll could even eclipse that of Jonestown.

In my view the international cult that has caused the most deaths worldwide due to doctrine is the Jehovah's Witnesses. The ban on blood transfusions has caused many needless deaths for more than 60 years. Organ transplants were also banned for a number of years by the Witness leaders and subsequently allowed in 1981. (For *more information see Losing The Faith: Truth under Scrutiny, Robin Jackson*)

Throughout history the search for the meaning of life has intrigued not only radical thinkers, but ordinary people intent on broadening their horizons. Repeated studies continue to indicate a wide and varied background for cult recruits.

Cults also emerge and seem to flourish out of the economic and social difficulties that exist in countries. South Africa's northern neighbour, Zimbabwe, a country suffering immense political and social misery has a classic example where a cult emerged out of the need to redress the country's cataclysmic stress. In the remote Guruve region, 140 kilometres north of Harare, the "Girl Jesus" saga is playing out. Tespy Nyanhete is reportedly to be between 11 and 13 years of age. Her parents, Okinibheti and Entrance Nyanhete, now known as Baba Josefa and Mai Maria are reportedly an offshoot of the Mudzimu Anoyera cult led by the late Emmanuel Mudyiwa dubbed the "Jesus of Chiweshe". Mudyiwa allegedly prophesied the birth of the girl as the "Third Voice of Jesus". He claimed to be the second.

Two years ago Tespy visited Harare with her parents to speak to Mugabe. This was refused and she subsequently went to the provincial governor's headquarters in Bindura. Although he was away her appearance caused a stir among the townspeople who were all desperate to catch a glimpse of the "Girl Jesus".

It was then reported that her followers were connected with the abduction of scores of children and that the help of international agencies were being called for to help with location, resettlement and rehabilitation of these children. Families seeking prosperity had given money and little girls to the cult. The children have shown signs of physical neglect and malnutrition.

In this example people are willing to give up their children to the cult in return for prosperity under conditions in a country that needs to redress widespread social misery.

Chapter 3

Cult Recruiting Techniques

A danger foreseen is half avoided.

Thomas Fuller

CULTS – How They Work

Robin Jackson

People join cults for different reasons. The popularity of so-called "accepted" religions is dwindling quite fast. A recent survey conducted in the United Kingdom reported that many of the mainstream religions have reported rapid decline in membership. This could very well be the trend here in South Africa, and the rest of the Western world. Interest in mysticism, new age teachings and the occult is certainly growing. More and more people are looking for a spiritual aspect to their lives. If mainstream religion fails to supply this then there are several cults around which appear to promise either guaranteed salvation, or at least a community of like-minded individuals.

There are numerous anti-cult groups that produce literature warning of the dangers of cult membership. There are also many ex-members who have written accounts about their time in a cult. Some, but not all, would argue that their lives have become more fulfilled by joining a cult. They may also say that their beliefs and way of life are just as valid as anybody else's. However, these groups continue to generate much criticism and to attract publicity (Believe me, some court it). This is likely to be adverse when their beliefs are practised in such a way that they not only contradict society's norms, but are sometimes illegal.

From my experience in a cult and the subsequent research conducted I, as well as other numerous resources, have noticed a pattern that is used by cults to recruit members. Young people are especially susceptible to cult recruiting techniques and are most often the target. Many cult watch groups such as the UK based INFORM and the American Cult Awareness Network tour schools and colleges informing people of the dangers and warning signs as to cult activity.

In 2000 authorities received complaints from families, theologians and ex-members that a controversial international cult was active in recruiting vulnerable youngsters on campuses in Cape Town and up-country. The International Churches of Christ (ICC) was outlawed from several UK and US universities for its alleged brainwashing and aggressive proselytising techniques, and for splitting up families. The Rand Afrikaans University banned the group in 1999 after receiving complaints. The University of Pretoria conducted an investigation into the group. Willem Nicol, who was campus priest said: "The ICC must be exposed. We didn't ban them simply because we did not want to give them publicity. They are a dangerous cult and youngsters need to be protected because they are not allowed to leave once they join."

On its website the ICC (not to be confused with the mainstream "Church of Christ") boasted of being active at Parow High School, University of Cape Town, University of the Western Cape and Cape Techinikon. Cults use every available means to gain new members, but why do people join cults? Four basic reasons have been identified.

† *Intellectual Reasons*

All of us have the ability to be intellectual and to use our reasoning processes. We are forever learning and seeking new ways to enrich our lives. In an unsure world, cults provide authoritative answers to questions that have plagued man for centuries: *Who am I? Why am I here? Where am I going? What does the future hold?* However, this does not mean they provide correct answers. Some provide a false sense of security with answers that play on people's ignorance. Cults prey on this ignorance and try to impress the uninformed with pseudo-scholarship.

The Way International's founder, Victor Paul Wierwille, quoted profusely from Hebrew and Greek to give the impression of scholarship. Jehovah's Witnesses give a similar impression when going from door to door.

† *Emotional Reasons*

Our emotional make-up allows us to experience emotions of joy, love, peace, happiness, kindness and other qualities. However, our emotional make-up also produces qualities of hatred, restlessness, depression, selfishness and so forth. In this way cults appeal to our basic emotional needs. We need a sense of meaningful direction and need to feel loved. Individuals who have emotional problems or have an identity crisis are particularly susceptible to being recruited into a cult. Low points in people's lives, such as the death of a loved one, are the opportunities that cults seek out to employ their recruitment techniques.

Cults take advantage of this and offer ready made solutions that are ultimately unsatisfying. The cults ultimately tell their followers what to think, how to behave and emphasize dependency on the group or leader for emotional stability.

† *Social Reasons*

People are not solitary beings but social ones. Our relationship to humanity is born from our social influence. We are active in society and fulfil our desire to be part of a group. When group-life is disrupted, because of a dysfunctional family, a bad church atmosphere, political issues or burn out at the workplace, people want to drop out of society and the cults are often there to catch them.

The cults also take advantage of other social factors such as when the hypocrisy of some religious leaders comes to the fore. They highlight these incidents and assure their followers that they have made the right move by joining them. However, when the groups own hypocrisy comes to the fore, or their leader's for that matter, these are hurriedly covered up or brushed aside as persecution.

† *Spiritual Reasons*

Many in today's society find themselves spiritually and morally lost. The collapse of religious values has regularly plagued humanity and is not a new phenomenon. That is partly the reason some look to alternative routes to faith and the meaning of existence. Interest in mysticism, new age teachings and the occult has become very popular in the West where spirituality has been eclipsed by the joys of wealth and material gratification. Some feel that mainstream religion is failing them and therefore they become easy prey for the cults.

Here are the techniques and some key warning signs that could indicate that a cult is trying to recruit you. Of course it may vary from cult to cult as to how these are applied. However, the basis is the same.

† *Hyped Meetings*

Instead of explaining to you upfront what the group believes or what their programme is, they will insist that you can only understand it by attending a group meeting. When you go to these meetings everyone around you seems so enthusiastic that you begin to wonder if there is something wrong with you. The environment they create is one where you feel so uncomfortable and the only way to become comfortable is to join in. This is an example of controlled peer pressure. This technique is especially used in commercial cults.

An acquaintance of mine related his experience to me where he was invited to attend one of these meetings. When he arrived everybody in the room was chanting and singing songs in unison. "The atmosphere was overwhelming", he said. Before he new it he had a bag of books in his hand which he was commissioned to sell from door to door with the promise of great wealth by following their special programme.

† *Intense and Unrelenting Pressure*

They will call on you repeatedly. Frequently they will meet you on campus, at your door or outside your place of work. They will trick you into going to their meetings for an hour but then lead you to a long study, meeting or talk. This intense and unrelenting pressure has to be kept up otherwise you might snap out of the mind control environment they are trying to immerse you in. One group calls this technique "Return Visits".

† *They Tell You They Are Not a Cult*

Most certainly this is a pre-emptive strike against the possible warnings you will get from friends and family which they know will come your way. Some cults will even tell you that Satan will send your friends and family to dissuade you from becoming involved with the "one true religion". This tactic often places a warped sense of logic in the new recruits mind. "The agents of Satan" eventually do come and warn him that it is a cult, so since the group predicted it, the group therefore must be true. Here I must stress, if any group tells you they are not a cult and that some people call them one, then for Pete's sake (and for yours of course) find out why!

Notice this extract from one of the publications that Jehovah's Witnesses use to indoctrinate recruits:

> Choosing God's friendship will put you at odds with the whole world. (John 15: 19) You may become the target of ridicule. Difficulties, problems, and temptations may assail you. But do not let anything rob you of your relationship with God. (Young People Ask... pg 318)

The above quote is from a book that the Watchtower uses to especially indoctrinate young people.

Recruiting is carried out with as little regard for truth as is collecting funds. They will say it is perfectly fine to use deception and some even encourage their followers to lie under oath in court when it comes to defending the cult's practises. The Moonies call it "Heavenly Deception". The Jehovah's Witnesses call it "Theocratic Strategy".

Steve Hassan, ex-Moonie and author of the book Combating Cult Mind Control says: "I have no qualms about referring to the Unification Church as a destructive cult." He should know, as he was recruited into the organization when he was at college. One of the Moonies recruiting techniques is to tell those having doubts that everyone will one day join the Unification Church — so they might as well join now.

In Dan Brown's novel, The Da Vinci Code, he describes a character by the name of Silas with the following words; 'He was broad and tall, with ghost-pale skin and thinning white hair. His irises were pink with dark red pupils.' This fictional Silas, the fanatic assassin, is a member of the organization called Opus Dei. This institution has been described over the years as a Catholic, ultraconservative, destructive cult. Opus Dei (The Work of God) was founded in 1928 by the Spanish priest José Maria Escrivá de Balaguer (Try saying that name after a few tequila shots!) Pope John Paul II canonized Escrivà on the 6th October 2002. Today the organization has spread to more than sixty countries partly due to its aggressive proselytising techniques. However, Escrivà's work, *The Way*, states that it does not welcome the masses into its ranks, but it employs a selective recruitment policy. Furthermore, in his *Constitutions of the Sacerdotal Society of the Holy Cross and Opus Dei* we read;

> To work with all our might so that the social class known as 'the intellectual' – which serves as a guide to the civil society due to its teachings, which have no equal, as well as due to the roles that it performs and the social prestige by which it distinguishes itself – embraces the precepts of Our Lord Jesus Christ and puts them into practice.

Therefore Opus Dei is different from most other cults in that it aims to attract the most capable, powerful, and educated individuals in society. Nevertheless, although it does concentrate on recruiting professionals and university graduates, it does address a more humble and less elitist public. Young people are approached at educational institutions. Institutions that depend entirely on Opus Dei are the organizations recruiting ground. However, those institutions that are guided by the spiritual directives of The Work also feature strongly in their recruitment drives.

Students who already are members of Opus Dei are usually employed in the role of recruitment agents. As soon as an individual is spotted and is ready for recruitment he is invited into the so-called Circle of Saint Raphael. Once the recruit is within the circle, meetings of fewer than ten people are arranged. The director of the Circle then explains certain Christian doctrinal issues from the viewpoint of the organization. As time goes by, the director then speaks with each new recruit individually and in private. This is how, by the use of persuasive techniques, the young recruit is led through the ranks of Opus Dei.

Members of Opus Dei are also required to practise self mortification of the body. Apart from having to wear a cilice belt (a leather strap studded with sharp metal barbs), they are required to use 'the discipline' (a heavy knotted rope that is slung over one's shoulder repeatedly) either on Saturday nights or on Sunday mornings.

Former Opus Dei member, Augustina López de los Mozos Muñoz writes in her testimony, *The Bitter Story of an Opus Dei Numerary*, which was published in Marie Claire magazine;

> I found out about 'the discipline' after a year and a half of being a member of The Work. This is a corporal mortification practice: a whip made out of a strong rope with several strands. It is used on Saturdays, only on Saturdays. You walk into the bathroom, you take off your underwear and then, kneeling down on the floor, you whip yourself on the buttocks for as long as it takes you to recite the 'Salve Regina' (or 'Hail Holy Queen') hymn prayer. I have to say that I would recite the 'Salve Regina' as fast as I possibly could, because the whipping on such a delicate part of the body would peel the skin off and leave the flesh bare, no matter how fast you were when reciting your prayer.

While members are being taught the practice of mortification of the body another more subtle practice takes place which is an identifying feature of all cults. The technique of mind control is employed.

Robin Jackson

Chapter 4

Mind Control — The Loaded Gun Technique

*The efficient man is the man who thinks for himself,
and is capable of thinking hard and long.*
Charles W. Eliot

CULTS – How They Work

Robin Jackson

Mind Control is not some mystical, magical, and invisible force that cults use to take away people's free will. Rather, it is a psychological technique that cult leaders attempt to control their members with. It does not turn people into some remote-controlled robot. In contrast, it is a dishonest influence placed very inconspicuously on cult members by the cult. So instead of Mind Control being some sort of irresistible force used to take over peoples minds, it is much more like a loaded gun. The cult leadership points the "gun" at a member and says "if you leave us you will lose all your friends and family", "if you don't conform you will go to hell", "if you don't give us money then you will fail in business." With reference to these three statements in the previous sentence, the only "live round" in that "gun" is the threat of loss of family and friends who are in the cult when a member wants to leave. The other two "rounds", in my opinion, are "blanks".

The technique of Mind Control can be broken up into several techniques too. However, collectively they make up the most deceptive means of controlling people's thoughts and actions.

Deception

Cults need to operate and recruit using deception. The reason for this is if people knew beforehand what their true practises are they would not join. They hide the truth from you until they think you are ready to accept it.

Imagine if the leader of the Heaven's Gate cult was open and honest about the group. Telling them outright that by joining the cult you would have to wear strange clothes, get castrated and drink poison, I doubt whether he would have had many takers.

Steve Hassan recalls how he was a disillusioned student, recently split from a girlfriend and desperately trying to find his way in life when he was approached by a group of people calling themselves the One World Crusade. It was only much later that he realised the group actually belonged to the Moonies.

Miguel Fisac, a member of Opus Dei for twenty years and a close observer of the organizations inner workings, outlines in his personal notes how he was personally recruited by the founder himself while enrolled at the DYA Academy. He was pressed to attend weekly sessions at which Escrivá would read from the Bible, talk about the necessity of observing Christian norms and reciting prayers. At no point during these sessions was reference made to Opus Dei. The introduction was done privately on a one-to-one basis. Escriviá then pretended he wanted to know more about his students and asked those who interested him to fill in a form giving biographic and personal information. When Fisac was asked to join he was caught completely off guard. He later wrote to a friend stating; 'I did not dare refuse, and it was a weakness that I began to regret the same day.'

To hide what the group is really like, cults normally have a very slick and well-rehearsed Public Relations front. This Public Relations front usually displays the image of an organization that helps the poor, supports research, the environment or peace. They will tell you how happy you will be in the group, but you will not be told what life really will be like. Moreover, nor will they tell you what they really believe. Introduction to these things is a slow and gradual process. You will not notice the change until you find yourself practicing and believing things that would have made you run a mile if you knew from the start.

A key point to remember is that no legitimate group needs to lie or mislead you about what they practice or believe.

Exclusivity

A common thread that runs through all cults and is a chief identifying mark of their mind control is the claim of being "the one true church". A normal religious organization would not have any problem with you moving to another similar organization as long as you stayed in that religion. This is because it is the belief system that matters, and not the membership to an organization. For instance, if you were a Christian then you could move from one church to another and still be a Christian.

However, cult leaders tell you that you can only be "saved" in their organization alone. All the others miss the mark and no other organization has the truth. An example of this can be found in the writings of The Church of Jesus Christ of Latter-day Saints:

> Every intelligent person under the heavens that does not, when informed, acknowledge that Joseph Smith, Jr., is a prophet of God, is in darkness and opposed to us and to Jesus and His kingdom on

47

earth (Brigham Young, Journal of Discourses, 8:223)

What does the Christian world know about God? Nothing...Why, so far as the things of God are concerned, they are the veriest fools; they know neither God nor the things of God. (John Taylor [Third president of the Mormon Church], Journal of Discourses, 13:225)

Martha Beck, ex-Mormon, life coach, and author of the book, *Leaving the Saints*, writes; "Mormons who leave the fold, unlike apostates from other faiths, tend to avoid joining any other church. I think there are two reasons for this: first, because Mormonism is so all-pervading, so exclusive of other creeds, and second, because Latter-day Saints are actually taught to test religious claims against their own sense of truth."

The Watchtower Society (Jehovah's Witnesses) also claims to be the only source for truth:

'It is God's sole collective channel for the flow of Biblical truth to men on earth.' (The Watchtower, July 15, 1960, p. 439)

Mary Baker Eddy, founder of Christian Science, also claimed sole collective channel for truth:

'Our Master...practised Christian healing...but left no definite rule for demonstrating this Principle of healing and preventing disease. This rule remained to be discovered by Christian Science.' (Science and Health, 147:24-29)

The Unification Church's leader, Sun Myung Moon claims exclusive knowledge:

'We are the only people who truly understand the heart of Jesus, and the hope of Jesus.' (Rev.Moon, The Way of the World, p.20)

The self styled leader and "evangelist" of the ICC's Cape Town branch, Werner Vos, made these remarks when interviewed:

"We are the only church that preaches the Bible. All others such as Catholics and Dutch Reformed are wrong. They don't know the Bible and are not biblical Christians like us."

The cult leaders need to make you believe there is nowhere else you can go and still be saved. If you ever leave the "one true church" then you are "going to hell", or "you will be destroyed" is what is often inscribed in the member's minds. This is a fear based control tactic designed to keep you in the cult. It also gives the cult leaders tremendous power over their recruits. They know that by you equating leaving the cult with leaving God (or leaving the only chance you have in succeeding in life), then you will obey the cult leaders even if you disagree with them.

Exclusivity is used as a threat. It is a way of controlling your behaviour through fear. Any group that says you must belong to their organization to be saved is almost certainly a cult. The bottom-line is, be very suspicious of a group that claims to be better than all the others, have a better grasp of the truth, and superior to the rest.

Intimidation

Cult leadership is often venerated and feared. The cult leadership will claim to have direct authority from God to control almost every aspect of your life. To disagree with the leadership is to disagree with God. If the cult is not religious then disagreeing with the leaders or the programme will still be seen as rebellious or stupid.

Guilt is often used to control you. Maybe the reason you're not making money is because you're not "with the programme". Maybe the reason you're not able to convert new recruits is because "you are puffed up with pride and full of sin". It could never be that the programme isn't working, or those new recruits have valid reasons for not joining. It's always your fault, you are always wrong, and so you must try harder. You will also be made to feel very guilty for disobeying any of the cult's written or unwritten rules.

One of the principle ways cults use to create guilt in you is by Character Assassination. This is false reasoning used by people or groups who have no real arguments.

I find the following given by a cult watch group to be a very good example of how Character Assassination works:

"One plus one equals three", says Ford
"No I don't think so. You see when I have one
thing, and I have another thing, then I have two
things not three", replies Arthur.
"I see your point, but what you must realize is that
one plus one when calculated in relation to this
complex number domain, which I just invented, and
then squared by the sum of the ninth tangent in the
sequence of the Fibonacci series results in three!",
stated Ford triumphantly.

Ok, Ford is wrong, but that is not the point. The
point is that Ford tried to answer Arthur's
reasoning with more reasoning of his own. This is
the healthy way people and groups debate subjects.
Now lets see what would have happened if Ford
had used Character Assassination...

"Arthur I have been a mathematician longer than

you. How dare you disagree with me! You are
obviously a very smug and prideful person. I think
you are disagreeing with me because you are
jealous of me, and to be honest with you Arthur,
your rebellion has really hurt me and a lot of other
people too", stated Ford his face intimidatingly
close to Arthur's.

You see Ford did not answer Arthur's argument. Instead he attacked Arthur's character. Character Assassination is a powerful tool to exert control over you.

The practise whereby one, two or three members of a cult attack the character of another person is called a breaking session. This can sometimes go on for hours and some cults will not stop until their victim breaks down in tears and cries uncontrollably.

Cult members therefore become fearful of disobeying or openly disagreeing with the cult leadership. In contrast, healthy organizations are not threatened by openly debating issues.

Relationship Control and Love-Bombing

We are profoundly affected by those around us, whether we like it or not. Cults know this and realise that if they control your relationships, then they can control you. When you first go to a cult meeting for the first time they will practice what is termed "love bombing". This is where you suddenly get instant friends.

According to testimonies from ex-Moonies their recruitment technique stretches to befriending people who seem likely to join. They then invite these potential new recruits for weekends away without once mentioning their association with the Moonies. Now surrounded by so-called friends, the new recruits are taken to a commune where they participate in games and a few soul searching seminars. However, most of the recruits will not be new at all, but are already converts who pretend to be at ease with revealing their darkest secrets and denouncing their parents. This form of "love bombing" would eventually wear down the most doubtful of people.

I recall a similar tactic used during my time with the Jehovah's Witnesses. Frequently Witnesses are encouraged, sometimes from the platform, that they should put on a happy face and welcome potential new members with open arms.

It will all seem so wonderful. How can such a loving group be wrong? However, you will soon learn that if you ever disagree with them or leave the cult you will lose all your so-called "friends". This unspoken threat influences your actions and thought process in a cult. Things that normally would have made you complain will pass by silently because you don't want to be ridiculed or ostracised. Like in an unhealthy relationship love is conditional. Cults hate others being able to influence you and therefore will try to cut you off from your friends and family. They will manoeuvre your life so as to maximise your contact with cult members and minimize your contact with people outside the group.

A point to take heed of here is to remember that true friendships develop over time. Beware of "instant friends". Be cautious of a group that tells you who you can and cannot see.

Information Control

Cults tell their members not to read any information outside the cult. All information from outside the cult is considered to be "evil", especially if that information is in opposition to the cult. Only information which is supplied by the cult is true. Here too cults label any information against it as "persecution" or "spiritual pornography". The cult I was a member of calls it "apostate literature". No doubt books like this one will likewise fall into their respective labels. You also run the risk of being expelled from the group if you are caught in possession of any such literature. Members are trained to instantly destroy any information critical of the cult, and not even to entertain the thought that it could be true.

Therefore, what we can conclude from this is that those who control the information control the person. Naturally, a person who does not consider all information will make unbalanced decisions. Throughout history the practice of filtering information available or trying to discredit it, not on the basis of how true it is, but how it supports the party-line is a common mind control tool.

This extract from the Watchtower's monthly publication, *Our Kingdom Ministry*, September 2007 edition, is a classic example of information control used by cults.

> *Does 'the faithful and discreet slave" endorse independent groups of Witnesses who meet together to engage in scriptural research or debate?*
>
> *No, it does not.* And yet in various parts of the world, a few associates of our organization have formed groups to do independent research on Bible-related subjects. [...] Throughout the earth, *Jehovah's people are receiving ample spiritual instruction* and encouragement at congregation meetings, assemblies, and conventions, as well as *through the publications of Jehovah's organization.* [...] *For those who wish to do extra Bible study and research, we recommend that they explore Insight on the Scriptures, "All Scripture Is Inspired Of God and Beneficial," and our other publications, such as those that discuss the prophecies found in the Bible books of Daniel, Isaiah, and Revelation.* These provide abundant

material for Bible study, [...] (September 2007, Kingdom Ministry, Question Box) [Emphasis mine]

In the above quote members are encouraged to only consult or research the Watchtowers publications for personal research purposes, thereby controlling the information they receive.

Another former Opus Dei member, Colm Larkin, explains how every book that could be read by Opus Dei members carried a censorship rating that ranged from one to six. Books that were rated with the number one could be read by everybody. Books rated with the number two could only be read if permission was granted. The books rated between three and five could only be read by established members and also depended on the amount of time they belonged to The Work. Lastly, those books rated with the number six were completely banned to everybody.

Legitimate groups have nothing to fear from their members reading critical information about them. The internet has become a valuable source of information. This tool has also proved to be a thorn in the side of many of these cults and they frequently discourage members from using it. Furthermore, I do admit that some information on the internet should be taken with a pinch of salt, but the vast majority of the information about cults is dead accurate.

In my opinion, any organization that has to constantly warn its followers against using the internet has a lot to hide. And certainly many of these groups would much rather cover-up much of their past (and present). If you are instructed by a group not to read any information critical of the group, then it is a sure sign of a cult.

Reporting Structures

In a mind control cult you must be careful what you say or do. "The walls have ears" and everyone is encouraged to look out for "struggling brothers and sisters". Cult members are then encouraged to report what they see to the leadership. Information, often given in strictest confidence, is reported to the leadership. This information is then used by the cult leadership to convince members that they have a supernatural link. The unsuspecting member does not realise there is a very natural mechanism behind the whole revelation.

The result is that people in a mind control cult will often hide their true thoughts and feelings. Instead they wear a figurative mask that presents them as the perfect cult member. The mask is a defence against being reported to leadership and being punished for not measuring up. Cult members never feel like they measure up to the cults ideals. They feel the others around them do, but in reality the others feel exactly the same way. The cults slowly build up an incredible edifice of dos and don'ts that the members try their best to meet, and the rest go on feeling guilty about because they cannot. The result is that cult members try to deceive outsiders, as well as fellow cult members.

Close friendships are also very rarely formed in cults. If they do, the cult leaders see this as a threat and very often move these people away from each other. Nothing is allowed that can be more powerful than the member's allegiance to the group and its leaders.

Time Control

Cults keep their members so busy with activities and meetings that the members do not have the time to think about their involvement. This also keeps them away from their family and friends and keeps them immersed in the cult environment. The International Society for Krishna Consciousness (ISKCON), better known as "Hare Krishna", demands a very strict routine from its fulltime members which some experts say could be seen as destructive. A typical day for a fulltime ISKCON member is as follows:

3 a.m. - Day starts with prayers.

4 a.m. – Service for the whole community followed by individual chanting till 6 a.m.

6 a.m. – Scripture study class takes place where the sacred text *The Bhagavad-Gita* is read until 7 a.m.

7.30 a.m. – Breakfast takes place followed by general communal chores until 10.a.m.

10 a.m. to 6 p.m. – Devotees are usually expected to sell books, spread the Hare Krishna message on the streets, and to help those in need, usually by offering free food.

6 p.m. – After a meal there will be more study and further services. Any remaining chores are also done before bedtime which is at 10 p.m.

The key point to remember here is that never-ending compulsory meetings and tasks is a sure sign that you are dealing with a cult.

We have seen how mind control is used as an effective tool to recruit, as well as control unsuspecting cult members. However, we must remember that people are not perfect, but if these techniques are constantly employed you are more than likely dealing with a cult.

Chapter 5

Profits from the Misfortune of Others

To do injustice is more disgraceful than to suffer it.

Plato

CULTS – How They Work

The pressure selling organizations and the multi-level marketing industry are some of the most common forms of commercial cults. They supposedly make money by selling products via their sales organization, but in actual fact they make their money by selling the products and motivational material to their sales organization. They need to constantly recruit new members to enhance their sales force, and hence their profits. And here's why this model causes controversy.

"And that's the trouble with multilevel marketing. You make money on your ability to use people. Once you sign on, you hardly have a choice. Not that you want anyone to fail, but you can't hit the jackpot unless you build the network, and that means signing up as many recruits as possible — most of whom have no chance of making the grade." (http://www.inc.com)

Their recruiters have to be very deceptive because of the bad reputation that some of these companies have. Some of these names are well known to the general public. Their method of recruitment often starts with a phone call asking to meet you to discuss a "business opportunity". Not once will they mention the organization behind it. This meeting will involve a long intense presentation carefully designed to try and convince you that you could make a lot of money by following their plan. They will bring in a highly charismatic speaker who will have you laughing, clapping, and stomping your feet. However, at the end of this highly entertaining presentation little would have been said on how to make it work. They might even bring up a bunch of people to give testimonials of how successful they have been. This is because testimonials are an easy substitute for statistical facts. They oversell the dream and undersell the business plan. Only near the end of the presentation will they mention the real name behind it. Bear in mind that this is deceptive. No legitimate business needs to use deception.

Robert L. Fitzpatrick, author of the book *False Profits*, has identified ten lies of the multi-level marketing industry in his twenty years of research.

- **Lie #1: MLM offers better opportunities than all other conventional business and professional models for making large amounts of money.**

Truth: For almost everyone who invests, MLM turns out to be a losing financial proposition. Less than 1% of all MLM distributors ever earn a profit and those earning a sustainable living at this business are a much smaller percentage still.

Extraordinary sales and marketing obstacles account for much of this failure, but even if the business were more feasible, sheer mathematics would severely limit the opportunity. The MLM business structure can support only a small number of financial winners. If a 1,000-person downline is needed to earn a sustainable income, those 1,000 will need one million more to duplicate the success. How many people can realistically be enrolled? Much of what appears as growth is in fact only the continuous churning of new enrolees. The money for the rare winners comes from the constant enrolment of armies of losers. With no limits on numbers of distributors in an area and no evaluation of market potential, the system is also inherently unstable.

- **Lie #2: Network marketing is the most popular and effective new way to bring products to market. Consumers like to buy products on a one-to-one basis in the MLM model.**

Truth: Personal retailing - including nearly all forms of door-to-door selling - is a thing of the past, not the wave of the future. Retailing directly to friends on a one-to-one basis requires people to drastically change their buying habits. They must restrict their choices, often pay more for goods, buy inconveniently, and engage in potentially awkward business relationships with close friends and relatives. In reality, MLM depends on reselling the opportunity to sign up more distributors.

- **Lie #3: Eventually all products will be sold by MLM. Retail stores, shopping malls, catalogues and most forms of advertising will soon be rendered obsolete by MLM.**

Truth: Less than 1% of all retail sales are made through MLM, and much of this is consists of purchases by hopeful new distributors who are actually paying the price of admission to a business they will soon abandon. MLM is not replacing existing forms of marketing. It does not legitimately compete with other marketing approaches at all. Rather, MLM represents a new investment scheme couched in the language of marketing. Its real products are distributorships that are sold through misrepresentation and exaggerated promises of income. People are buying products in order to secure positions on the sales pyramid. The possibility is always held out that you may become rich if not from your own efforts then from some unknown person ("the big fish") who might join your "downline."

- MLM's growth does not reflect its value to the economy, customers, or distributors, but the high levels of economic fear, insecurity, wishes for quick and easy wealth. The market dynamics are similar to those of legalized gambling, but the percentage of winners is much smaller.

- **Lie #4: MLM is a new way of life that offers happiness and fulfilment. It provides a way to attain all the good things in life.**

Truth: The most prominent motivational themes of the MLM industry, as shown in industry literature and presented at recruitment meetings, constitute the crassest form of materialism. Fortune 100 companies would blush at the excess of promises of wealth, luxury, and personal fulfilment put forth by MLM solicitors. These appeals actually conflicts with most people's true desire for meaningful and fulfilling work at something in which they have special talent or interest.

- **Lie #5: MLM is a spiritual movement.**

Truth: The use of spiritual concepts like prosperity, consciousness and creative visualization to promote MLM enrolment, the use of words like "communion" to describe a sales organization, and claims that MLM fulfils Christian principles or Scriptural prophecies are great distortions of these spiritual practices. Those who focus their hopes and dreams upon wealth as the answer to their prayers lose sight of genuine spirituality as taught by religions. The misuse of these spiritual principles should be a signal that the investment opportunity is deceptive. When a product is wrapped in the flag or in religion, buyers beware! The "community" and "support" offered by MLM organizations to new recruits is based entirely upon their purchases. If the purchases and enrolment decline, so does the "communion."'

- **Lie #6: Success in MLM is easy. Friends and relatives are the natural prospects. Those who love and support you will become your life-time customers.**

Truth: The commercialization of family and friendship and the use of "warm leads" advocated in MLM marketing programs are a destructive element in the community and very unhealthy for individuals involved. People do not appreciate being pressured by friends and relatives to buy products. Trying to capitalizing upon personal relationships to build a business can destroy one's social foundation.

- **Lie #7: You can do MLM in your spare time. As a business, it offers the greatest flexibility and personal freedom of time. A few hours a week can earn a significant supplemental income and may grow to a very large income, making other work unnecessary.**

Truth: Making money in MLM requires extraordinary time commitment as well as considerable personal skill and persistence. Beyond the sheer hard work and talent required, the business model inherently consumes more areas of one's life and greater segments of time than most occupations. In MLM, everyone is a prospect. Every waking moment is a potential time for marketing. There are no off-limit places, people, or times for selling. Consequently, there is no free space or free time once a person enrols in MLM system. While claiming to offer independence, the system comes to dominate people's entire life and requires rigid conformity to the program. This is why so many people who become deeply involved end up needing and relying upon MLM desperately. They alienate or abandon other sustaining relationships.

- **Lie #8. MLM is a positive, supportive new business that affirms the human spirit and personal freedom.**

Truth: MLM is largely fear-driven. Solicitations inevitably include dire predictions about the impending collapse of other forms of distribution, the disintegration or insensitivity of corporate America, and the lack of opportunity in other occupations. Many occupations are routinely demeaned for not offering" unlimited income." Working for others is cast as enslavement for "losers." MLM is presented as the last best hope for many people. This approach, in addition to being deceptive, frequently discourages people who otherwise would pursue their own unique visions of success and happiness. A sound business opportunity does not have to base its worth on negative predictions and warnings.

- **Lie #9. MLM is the best option for owning your own business and attaining real economic independence.**

Truth: MLM is not true self-employment. "Owning" an MLM distributorship is an illusion. Some MLM companies forbid distributors to carry other companies' products. Most MLM contracts make termination of the distributorship easy and immediate for the company. Short of termination, downlines can be taken away arbitrarily. Participation requires rigid adherence to a "duplication" model, not independence and individuality. MLM distributors are not entrepreneurs but joiners in a complex hierarchical system over which they have little control.

- **Lie #10: MLM is not a pyramid scheme because products are sold.**

Truth: The sale of products does not protect against anti-pyramid-scheme laws or unfair trade practices set forth in federal and state law. MLM is a legal form of business only under rigid conditions set forth by the FTC and state attorneys general. Many MLMs are violating these guidelines and operate only because they have not been prosecuted. Recent court rulings are using a 70% rule to determine an MLM's legality: At least 70% of all goods sold by the MLM company must be purchased by nondistributors. This standard would place most MLM companies outside the law. The largest MLM acknowledges that only 18% of its sales are made to nondistributors.

Recently a well known national radio station in South Africa featured a discussion slot on the multi-level marketing industry. People were invited to call in and relate their experiences with these companies. The vast majority of callers echoed the very same sentiments stating that it was not very profitable for them getting involved in these companies. However, there were a few callers who had positive comments and who stated that they had seen good profits by following the MLM programmes.

Cultwatch advises that you should ask the recruiter the following key questions:

- **Is it XZY group?** Ask them if they are, or are involved with any of the well known commercial cults. Often the recruiter will admit to some connection, and in fact the clever recruiter will plainly state their involvement rather than having their deception uncovered later on.

- **Could I see some properly certified audited accounts which demonstrate this business model working?**

CULTS – How They Work

Like any business they should be able to provide the hard numbers. Not stories of other people making it big, or generalizations about six figure incomes, or more enthusiastic claims that you can make it if you work hard enough.

- **If this is a new business can I see a business plan, profit and loss projections for the next year, two years and** five years? If they claim it is a successful established business then demand to see the books. These are not unreasonable demands, as no successful business person would ever touch a venture without this basic information.

- **Could I run them past my own accountant and my lawyer too?** If it's for real then they will be more than happy to comply, otherwise watch them squirm and dodge with all manner of well rehearsed excuses. If they do produce the information then go to your accountant, you're a fool if you don't.

Most people are not only money motivated, but are money desperate. Due to this fact they can be easy targets for people selling the "dream". Naturally we would want to make more money while working less. However, the pressure selling and multi-level marketing organizations will rarely make good on this promise. It's just not as easy as they want you to believe.

Many of these companies are perceived as leaches because they are structured to profit from the misfortune of others. Not that they want people to fail, but is inevitable that most will. The majority of the people in the world are just not cut out to be good salesmen or saleswomen. The companies know this and continue to recruit to fuel the growth of the company and the profits of the elite few at the top.

Furthermore, multilevel marketing is a legitimate and legal business model. It has also proven to be successful by many companies in a number of different industries. As with any business model, those people who are qualified, passionate, and determined will be successful. However, the vast majority of people are not. Be careful of becoming too infatuated by the dream that you allow yourself to believe anything.

The pressure selling technique is not only used by commercial cults. The religious cults use a similar technique. Former Moonie, Steve Hassan, and other critics have stated that Moon is keen to recruit young people because they will work hard for him. The church's wealth has been built up by the devoted labour of members. As soon as they have joined, the Moonies are told they must make money for the organization. Moonies do not recruit while they are selling. Instead they are notorious for their devious methods of raising funds on the streets, and often go from door to door selling pictures and plants. They will not disclose where the money is going and will lie if asked. Of course, Moon says this is fine (Heavenly Deception).

Jehovah's Witnesses are known for their door to door work and peddling of Watchtower literature. Moreover, members try to win over new recruits by offering a "free home Bible study" to householders. Each Witness is then required to fill in report slips each month detailing what "witnessing" activity was done. These reports list how many hours were spent going from door to door, the amount of literature distributed and so forth. Former Jehovah's Witness and Governing Body member, Raymond Franz, writes with regard to these report cards in his book *Crisis of Conscience*:

'The importance given to these reports is undeniable. Every Witness reports to the congregation, every congregation reports to the Branch Office of their country, every Branch Office sends a detailed monthly report to the international headquarters where these monthly reports are compiled, averages are figured, percentages of increase are noted. They are studied with the same avid interest that a large corporation would study the figures of its production records, its business growth; any fluctuations or downward trends in the number of Witnesses reporting time, the hours reported or the distribution of literature becomes cause for concern. Branch representatives become uneasy if the monthly reports for their country fail to show increase or, worse, show a decrease.'(*Crisis of Conscience, footnote, pg 293*)

The elders in the congregations of Jehovah's Witnesses are frequently instructed to visit and "counsel" the "inactive" members to get back into the "field service" and start "reporting time". Of course, this only serves as a means of getting sales up for the big Watchtower publishing corporation.

The ICC persuades new recruits to move into one of their communal homes and are told to hand over ten percent of student grants or income from jobs and families. They are then sent out to recruit new members. Daily targets are set which if not met result in humiliation, threats and bullying.

Many other groups use similar tactics. The end result is always the same. In my view, these organizations make billions of dollars by effectively using cheap labour.

Robin Jackson

Chapter 6

Prophecies, Signs and Wonders

When a prophet speaketh in the name of the Lord, if the thing follow not, nor come to pass, that is the thing which the Lord hath not spoken, but the prophet hath spoken it presumptuously: thou shalt not be afraid of him.

Deuteronomy 18: 22 (King James Version)

CULTS – How They Work

The leaders of cults often attempt to prove their "anointing" with prophecies of future events or special signs, such as healing, or wonders such as miraculous events. Certainly the list has proved to be long.

The apostles and prophets of the Mormon Church have made several dated predictions of future events. The Watchtower Bible and Tract Society, beginning with their founder Charles Taze Russell, have predicted the date of Christ's return and the beginning of the battle of Armageddon. The founder of the Worldwide Church of God, Herbert W. Armstrong, has made several predictions as to world events. The Christian Scientists boldly published *A Century of Christian Science Healings,* announcing the healings of hundreds of people through Mary Baker Eddy's methods. The Way International boasted of signs and wonders, including people raised from the dead. The followers of Sun Myung Moon are immersed in visions of the "True Parents" (Moon and his wife) during prayer. The New Age cults and Unity School speak of astonishing healings that defy explanation. Transcendental Meditation devotees, Siddhis, claim the miraculous events of walking through walls and levitation.

Are these people really giving accurate predictions and prophecies? Are these events miraculous? No doubt these events do hold a tight grip on the lives of many cult members who believe that these signs are "proof of God's blessing".

Some of these "signs and wonders" and so-called miraculous events will actually happen. They will be no more than slight of hand tricks by refined showmen. Case in point was the charismatic and influential leader of The People's Temple cult, Jim Jones. The cult gained notoriety, and new members, because of Jim Jones's "hands-on" healing sessions. Jones would withdraw cancerous growths and other visible ailments from members who came to him for help. The cancers would subsequently be displayed in a handkerchief. It was later revealed, by former followers of Jones, that the healing sessions were carefully planned staged dramas and that the "cancers" extracted from the individuals were actually animal parts such as chicken guts. (This slight-of-hand trick is still employed by many "psychic surgeons.")

Transcendental Meditation claims to teach people how to meditate and ultimately to fly. They also, allegedly can levitate, walk through walls and even become invisible. There are photographs, issued by the movement of course, of this "yogic flying," but it has to be said they do resemble cross-legged people who have either developed the ability to bounce or are aided by a trampoline which is just out of shot. Furthermore, TM organizations in the USA had to pay an ex-member substantial damages in 1987 when he filed a suit against them. He claimed TM did not reduce stress or improve his memory, and did not teach him to fly.

Joseph Smith, founder of the Church of Jesus Christ of Latter-day Saints has been the subject of some controversy. Apart from the false prophecies made by Smith, his writings were also fraudulent. One example of this is the bound volume of work called the Pearl of Great Price. It contains five sections: *The Book of Moses*, the *Book of Abraham, Joseph*

Smith-Matthew, *Joseph Smith-History*, and the *Articles of Faith*. The Book of Abraham is of particular interest as it is supposed to be a translation of an Egyptian papyrus that rewrites Genesis chapter 1 as "the gods" create instead of "God".

Controversy has swirled around this book since Smith introduced it in 1835. It all started when Michael Chandler of New York toured the American countryside charging admission to observers to see eleven Egyptian mummies that had been buried with rolls of papyrus. These had been willed to Mr Chandler and when he arrived in Kirtland, Ohio, Joseph Smith purchased the mummies from Chandler. Smith began to translate the hieroglyphics of the papyri and *"much to our joy found that one of the rolls contained the writings of Abraham, another the writings of Joseph of Egypt"* (*History of the Church*, *2:236*). The resulting translation of one of the papyri was accepted as scripture by the Mormons, the *Book of Abraham*.

However, in 1967 the collection of papyrus that formed the *Book of Abraham* had been rediscovered in the Metropolitan Museum in New York. This gave Egyptologists a fresh look at the writings of Joseph Smith. To the disappointment of the Mormon Church not a single Egyptologists confirmed a single word in Smith's translation. Even more disappointing was that the papyri had nothing to do with Abraham, but only contained burial instructions for a common Egyptian funeral. Smith's translation therefore proved to be of a fraudulent nature.

The Watchtower Society is probably the organization that has predicted more dates than any other in history. I will give examples of dates projected as false prophecies.

- **1874** – 'The Millennial Day; the Day of the Lord's rest, following the six thousand years of evil which ended in 1874' (*Studies in the Scriptures*, 7:301)

- **1914** – 'The 'battle of the great day of God Almighty' (Revelation 16:14), which will end in A.D. 1914 with the complete overthrow of earth's present rulership'(ibid.,2:101)

- **1915** – 'The end of the time of the gentiles, referred to in the text above, was reprinted with a new date, "which will end in A.D. 1915 with the complete overthrow of earth's present rulership' (ibid., 1914 ed).

- **1918** – 'The end of the times of the gentiles was recalculated with new dates in the seventh volume of *Studies*, "and in the light of the foregoing Scriptures, prove that the Spring of 1918 will bring upon Christendom a spasm of anguish greater ever than that experienced in the Fall of 1914. Reexamine the table of the Parallel Dispensations in *Studies in the Scriptures*, Vol. 2, and 1914 to 1918, and we believe it is correct and will be fulfilled ' with great power and glory' (ibid., 7:62)

- **1920** – 'The fleshly apostates from Christianity – shall be utterly desolated, 'even all of it.' Not one vestige of it shall survive the ravages of world-wide all-embracing anarchy, in the fall of 1920'(ibid.,7:542)

- **1925** – 'Based upon the argument heretofore set forth... that 1925 shall mark the resurrection of the faithful worthies of old... we must reach the positive and indisputable conclusion that millions now living will never die.' (*Millions Now Living Will Never Die*, Rutherford, 1920, pg. 97)

- **1942** – 'Those faithful men of old may be expected back from the dead any day now... In this expectation the house in at San Diego, California... was built, in 1930, and named 'Beth- Sarim'...It is now held in trust for the occupancy of those princes on their return' (*The New World*, Rutherford,1942, pg. 104).

- **1975** – 'In view of the short period of time left, we want to do this [pioneer work] as often as circumstances permit. Just think, brothers, there are only about 90 months left [until October 1975] before 6000 years of man's existence on earth is completed' (*Kingdom Ministry*, March 1968, pg.4)

- **1980** – 'It is possible that A.D. 1980 marks the regathering of all fleshly Israel from their captivity in death. It is just 70 years beyond 1910, the date when Pastor Russell gave his great witness to the Jewish people.' (*Studies in the Scriptures*, 7:62)

Not one of the Watchtower Society's predicted dates have ever come true. Furthermore, you would think that based on the evidence presented to cult members exposing inconsistencies and blatant forgery on the part of the leadership that members would up and leave. Some do, but for the majority it is not that easy. Many psychologists believe that when the mind is faced with such inconsistencies, it tries to restore consistency. It now tries to reinterpret the situation so as to minimize whatever inconsistencies that may be there. The term "cognitive dissonance" comes to mind.

Chapter 7

Cognitive Dissonance-Easier Left than Said

"In the long run it is far more dangerous to adhere to illusion than to face what the actual fact is."

Physicist David Bohm

The first question that many cult members ask when confronted with the truthfulness of the cult is; "Where else would I go?" It may appear to be a valid question but at the time of questioning it is a mental diversion from a topic being discussed. It is a 'thought stopping' technique. "Where else to go" is of no relevance until there is a thorough understanding of a more important question; "Does the cult promote truth?"

Fear should not prevent an honest evaluation of the facts about a group. It is only once you are convinced that the cult does not teach truth and is dishonest, that a person can rightfully address the question "Where to now?" Moreover the question is not unique to one particular cult. Doubting members of the Mormons, Worldwide Church of God, Moonies, and Jehovah's Witnesses all echo the very same sentiment. Steve Hassan refers to this as Phobia Indoctrination and says "members are systematically made to be phobic about ever leaving the group" (Combating Cult Mind Control, page 45, Steven Hassan, Park Street Press, 1990). This fear is the reason for the success the cults have in keeping people from facing the truth about the group.

Professor Daniel Taylor, author of *The Myth of Certainty*, writes in his book;

> '*Nonetheless, questioning the institutions is synonymous, for many, with attacking God—something not long to be tolerated. Supposedly they are protecting God . . . Actually, they are protecting themselves, their view of the world, and their sense of security. ... This threat is often met, or suppressed even before it arises, with power. . . Institutions express their power most clearly by enunciating, interpreting and enforcing the rules of the subculture.*'

Taylor's comments explain why religions can become oppressive to the point of excommunication, war or crusade.

When confronted with this dilemma the mind suffers from what is termed *cognitive dissonance*. It is safer mentally to refuse to consider the implications of such inconsistencies of belief than to confront them. If a person confronts these inconsistencies and realises that what they were taught was wrong, they are faced with the fact that many years of their lives has been spent in pointless pursuits and end up not knowing what to do next.

This philosophical question is paralleled in the movie *The Matrix* written by Andy and Larry Wachowski.

> <u>Neo</u>: *What truth?*
> <u>Morpheus</u>: *That you are a slave, Neo. Like everyone else, you were born into bondage, born inside a prison that you cannot smell, taste, or touch. A prison for your mind. (long pause, sighs) Unfortunately, no one can be told what the Matrix is. You have to see it for yourself. This is your last chance. After this, there is no turning back.*
> *(In his left hand, Morpheus shows a blue pill.)*

Morpheus: You take the blue pill and the story ends. You wake in your bed and believe whatever you want to believe. (A red pill is shown in his other hand) You take the red pill and you stay in Wonderland and I show you how deep the rabbit-hole goes. (Long pause; Neo begins to reach for the red pill) Remember, all I am offering is the truth, nothing more.

Cognitive dissonance is not a dilemma that can be solved that easily, as is seen in the study of a cult that was awaiting the end of the world. The founder of the cult stated that she had received a message from the "Guardians" of outer space that there would be an enormous flood on a certain day. On midnight of the appointed day only the true believers would be picked up by a spacecraft and will be saved. (Okay, since the days of Noah's Ark technology has advanced quite a bit you know!) The members of the sect gathered on "doomsday" and waited for the predicted catastrophe. The time of the spacecraft's arrival came and went and still no spacecraft was in sight. Tension now started to mount as the clock ticked on and still no spacecraft or flood arrived. Finally, the leader of the cult received another message. This time she said that to reward the faith of the faithful, the world was saved. The members were ecstatic and became more faithful than ever.

One might expect the very opposite given the failure of the prophecy. It should presumably lead one to abandon the beliefs that produced the prediction. However, the cognitive dissonance theory says otherwise. If the person were to abandon the belief that there are Guardians he would have to accept a painful dissonance between his present scepticism and his past beliefs and actions. His past belief would now appear extremely foolish. In retrospect, giving up their jobs and spending their life savings would lose all meaning without the belief in the Guardians. Under the new circumstances and the "new message" the dissonance was intolerable. It was reduced by a belief in the "new message" which reinforced the original belief. They could now think of themselves, not as fools, but as loyal and courageous members whose steadfast faith saved the earth.

For many it is easier to take the figurative *blue pill* and think no further as to what they believe is truth. Those who are brave enough and whose desire for real truth becomes too strong to ignore, end up taking the figurative *red pill*. It very often takes an enormous amount of courage to finally step outside of the insular world of a cult. From the outside looking in you begin to see just how deep the rabbit hole really goes.

Chapter 8

Leaving the Cults

Change is not made without inconvenience, even from worse to better.

Richard Hooker

The issue that the majority of former cult members will agree on is that there is no easy way to exit from a cult. For some, it is not that difficult to leave. They are just less susceptible to mind control techniques. Some maintain that sense of self to make an informed decision to leave. There are many ex-cultists who say they spent years working up the nerve to get out. It really does take a tremendous amount of courage to leave and believe me it doesn't come easy. To the cult member it will result in alienation from friends and family who might still be in the cult, and starting all over again. The person has to literally pick up the pieces when they leave. They have to try and renew old friendships and ties with family members they have cut off years before.

A peaceful, voluntary method of leaving a cult is certainly the preferred method but it doesn't always happen that way. When sixteen members of The Peoples Temple in Jonestown, Guyana, decided they wanted to leave the cult in 1978 following a visit by the U.S. government group, several armed cult members followed them to the airport and opened fire. A United States congressman, Leo Ryan, was killed along with three reporters and cult members. Eleven others were injured in the attack. Jim Jones, leader of the cult, feared the repercussions of the attack and initiated a mass suicide and murder of more than 900 people.

The consequences of leaving a cult very often results in the individual being shunned and former cult friends and family are no longer allowed to speak with, or associate with the cult leaver. These former members are often given labels such as "apostates" and their character is very often assassinated. The Watchtower organization certainly advocates a breaking of family ties from the one who has been disfellowshipped or chose to leave the organization.

Questions from Readers

• In the case of where a father or mother or son or daughter is disfellowshiped, how should such person be treated by members of the family in their family relationship?—P.C., Ontario, Canada.

We are not living today among theocratic nations where such members of our fleshly family relationship could be exterminated for apostasy from God and his theocratic organization, as was possible and was ordered in the nation of Israel in the wilderness of Sinai and in the land of Palestine.

Being *limited by the laws* of the worldly nation in which we live and also by the laws of God through Jesus Christ, we can take action against apostates *only to a certain extent, that is, consistent with both sets of laws.* The law of the land and God's law through Christ *forbid us to kill apostates, even though they be members of our own flesh-and-blood family relationship.* However, God's law requires us to recognize their being disfellowshiped from his congregation, and this despite the fact that the law of the land in which we live requires us under some natural obligation to live with and have dealings with such apostates under the same roof.

Of course, if the children are of age, then there can be a departing and breaking of family ties in a physical way, because the spiritual ties have already snapped.

(Nov 15, 1952 Watchtower pp.703-704 Questions from Readers) [Italics mine]

It certainly is a harsh view that is being advocated in this passage and all too often has been the cause of rifts between family members.

One of the major objectives of cults is to create a physical and psychological rift between its members and the outside world. To leave or even speak out against a cult is risky as you risk being excommunicated or suffer mental and physical abuse. This can take many forms. In the extreme it may result in the assassination of the ex-cult member. Case in point is the murder of Aston Green who was a member of the Nation of Yahweh cult lead by Yahweh Ben Yahweh. Green decided to leave the cult but went to the temple building to pick up his Bible before attempting to escape. He was beaten to the point of death by a group of about ten cult members. Following the brutal beating they took him to a wasteland where he was beheaded.

Psychological pressure is more commonplace. In one case a coffin bearing the name of the person being victimised was paraded past their house. Years of abuse can very well follow the leaving of a cult. This is most common from members living in the same neighbourhood.

Generally there are three ways that you can leave a cult. The first way is the voluntary route. People who leave on their own have normally re-evaluated the nature of the group and have come to their own conclusions. Independent research into the group from outside sources have helped many to see the deception and often come to the knowledge of cover-ups and information that the cult does not want their rank and file to have access to. Many former cult members have written accounts about their time spent in a cult and this can be a valuable resource for those contemplating leaving a cult. Some are not that susceptible to the mind control techniques employed by the cults and make an informed decision to leave. However, making the decision to leave is only part of the process. The cult has to "unlock the door" so the individual can leave. This is easier said than done. Some destructive cults will allow people to leave but they put a lot of pressure on you to stay.

The second way people leave a cult is by intervention. This is normally done when concerned family members or friends hope to rescue an individual from a destructive cult. De-programming is usually a method employed by some counsellors but is nowadays frowned upon. This method is synonymous with the initial kidnapping of the member from the cult setting. It then involves hours and hours of "debriefing" whereby a team of deprogrammers hold the cult member against his or her will. They then use ethical psychological techniques to counter the unethical psychological techniques used by the cult. The goal is to get the cult member to think for himself and to re-evaluate his situation.

Debriefing methods usually include educating the cult member on thought reform techniques and to help him to recognise those methods in his own cult experience. It also involves asking the cult member questions that help him to think in a critical and independent way so that it helps him to recognize that kind of thinking and praising him for it. Furthermore it helps to establish an emotional connection to his former life by introducing objects from his past and having family members relate past memories of his pre-cult life.

Cult expert and clinical psychologists, Margaret Singer, defined deprogramming simply as "providing members with information about the cult and showing them how their own decision-making power had been taken away from them" ("Cults in Our Midst" 1995).

During the 1970s deprogramming was a relatively common practice. Today it has fallen out of favour as an acceptable "cult busting" technique. It is a very costly exercise and has led to a lot of lawsuits over the years because of the practise of kidnapping and imprisonment of cult members. It is for this reason that many turn to exit counsellors instead. Exit counselling leaves out the kidnapping part and rather employs psychological techniques that might get the member to agree to voluntary debriefing. Voluntary exit counselling has to be adapted carefully to meet the individual's needs.

In 2005 a teenager from Northcliff, Johannesburg, South Africa, had to be rescued from the grips of a cult called The Living Love Fellowship .The girl ran away from home and married the self-styled mystical leader named Amadon. She was then taken from South Africa to a farm in Oregon, United States, where the cult was based. The family subsequently contacted a former policeman to help rescue the girl from the cult. Working closely with the authorities in the US the policeman then travelled to the cult's base in Oregon where they confronted Amadon.

At first the cult leader refused them access to see the girl. After repeatedly threatening to arrest him and to charge him with possession of pornography, they were allowed to see the girl in her room. When told that she had to go with them the girl did not even argue or resist. She immediately packed her things and left after Amadon had given them her passport.

From their observations they concluded that the girl was definitely being kept against her will. It was also then revealed that the girl had to work on the farm and had been sexually abused. She had to receive extensive counselling after the ordeal.

Luke Lamprecht, cult expert and corporate manager for the Teddy Bear Clinic, a centre for sexually abused children in South Africa, has helped to infiltrate many cults in South Africa and by virtue of experience, painted a bleak picture of the Living Love Fellowship. He says the teachings of the LLF are nothing but "idle ramblings" that would appeal to teenage anguish.

The third way that people leave a cult is when the cult kicks a member out because of so-called wrongdoing on the part of the cult member. This wrongdoing can range from legitimate crimes to deeds perceived only by the cult as offences. "Offences" such as reading literature opposing the cult, questioning the leadership or doctrines, and refusing to follow the orders of the leadership can lead to members being thrown out of the cult.

For many, leaving a cult is like experiencing the death of a close relative or a broken relationship. The feeling is often described as being betrayed by someone you were in love with. You feel as if you were simply used.

The following passage is how former cult members and those coming out of spiritually abusive systems described how they felt when they finally left their group.

"IT HURTS"

IT HURTS *to discover you were deceived - that what you thought was the "one true religion," the "path to total freedom," or "truth" was in reality a cult.*

IT HURTS *when you learn that people you trusted implicitly - whom you were taught not to question - were "pulling the wool over your eyes" albeit unwittingly.*

IT HURTS *when you learn that those you were taught were your "enemies" were telling the truth after all -- but you had been told they were liars, deceivers, repressive, satanic etc and not to listen to them.*

IT HURTS *when you know your faith in God hasn't changed - only your trust in an organization - yet you are accused of apostasy, being a trouble maker, a "Judas". It hurts even more when it is your family and friends making these accusations.*

IT HURTS *to realize their love and acceptance was conditional on you remaining a member of good standing. This cuts so deeply you try and suppress it. All you want to do is forget - but how can you forget your family and friends?*

IT HURTS *to see the looks of hatred coming from the faces of those you love - to hear the deafening silence when you try and talk to them. It cuts deeply when you try and give your child a hug and they stand like a statue, pretending you aren't there. It stabs like a knife when you know your spouse looks upon you as demonised and teaches your children to hate you.*

IT HURTS *to know you must start all over again. You feel you have wasted so much time. You feel betrayed, disillusioned, suspicious of everyone including family, friends and other former members.*

IT HURTS *when you find yourself feeling guilty or ashamed of what you were - even about leaving them. You feel depressed, confused, lonely. You find it difficult to make decisions. You don't know what to do with yourself because you have so much time on your hands now - yet you still feel guilty for spending time on recreation.*

IT HURTS *when you feel as though you have lost touch with reality. You feel as though you are "floating" and wonder if you really are better off and long for the security you had in the organization and yet you know you cannot go back.*

IT HURTS *when you feel you are all alone - that no one seems to understand what you are feeling. It hurts when you realize your self confidence and self worth are almost non-existent.*

IT HURTS *when you have to front up to friends and family to hear their "I told you so" whether that statement is verbal or not. It makes you feel even more stupid than you already do - your confidence and self worth plummet even further.*

IT HURTS *when you realize you gave up everything for the cult - your education, career, finances, time and energy - and now have to seek employment or restart your education. How do you explain all those missing years?*

IT HURTS *because you know that even though you were deceived, you are responsible for being taken in. All that wasted time........ at least that is what it seems to you - wasted time.*

This gives you a bit of insight into their pain and why there are no easy answers for them. The emotions they experience are varied and include feelings of guilt, depression, anger, mistrust, disillusionment and grief. To better cope with these emotions it is best to seek professional help and counselling from experts in the field.

Yes, it hurts. But it will heal with time and understanding. In time the negative feelings will be replaced with clear thinking, trust and peace. Your life will revert back to normal and you may even renew old friendships and family ties you broke because of your involvement in the cult. You may find that many of them will be glad to renew acquaintances after years of no contact. As a former cult member, trust me, there is life after the cult.

APPENDIX

A partial list of books recommended and cited for individuals needing more information and support in escaping from cults.

Abuse

- In the Name of Love: Abusive Controlling Relationships (DVD)

- The Battered Woman Dr. Lenore Walker (Perennial; Reprint edition, May 30, 1980)

- Breaking the Cycle of Abuse: How to Move beyond Your Past to Create an Abuse-Free Future Beverly Engel (John Wiley & Sons Inc., 2005)

- Emotional Blackmail: When the People in Your Life Use Fear, Obligation and Guilt to Manipulate You Susan Forward & Donna Frazier (Harper Paperbacks April 1, 1998)

- Emotional Vampires: Dealing with People who Drain You Dry Albert J. Bernstein (McGraw-Hill, 2000)

- The Emotionally Abused Woman : Overcoming Destructive Patterns and Reclaiming Yourself M.F.C.C. Beverly Engel (Ballantine Books, Reissue edition 1992)

- Father's Touch, Second Edition Donald D'Haene (LTI Publishing, Inc.; 2nd edition October 2004)

- In Sheeps Clothing: Understanding and Dealing with Manipulative People George K Simon (A.J. Christopher, 1996)

- More Than Victims: Battered Women Syndrome, Society, and the Law Donald Alexander Downs (University of Chicago Press, 1996)

- People Who Play God: How Ultra-Authorities Enslave the Hearts, Minds, Souls of Their Victims Beth E. Peterson (Xlibris Corp., 2003)

- Saving Beauty From the Beast: How to Protect Your Daughter from an Unhealthy Relationship Vicki Crompton, Ellen Zelda Kessner (Little Brown & Company, 2003)

- The Secret of Overcoming Verbal Abuse: Getting Off the Emotional Roller Coaster and Regaining Control of Your Life Albert Ellis and Marcia Grad Powers (Wilshire Book Company, 2000)

- Sex in the Forbidden Zone Rutter, Peter, M.D (Fawcett; Reprint edition October 21, 1991)

- Shattered: Six Steps from Betrayal to Recovery Fay A. Kingler, Bettyanne Bruth (Mappletree Publishing Company 2005)

- Surviving Domestic Violence, Voices Of Women Who Broke Free Ed.D. Weiss Elaine (Agreka Books, 2000)

- Surviving Intimate Terrorism Hedda Nussbaum (Publish America September 12, 2005)

- Take Back Your Life: Recovering from Cults and Abusive Relationships Janja Lalich, Madeleine Landau Tobias (Bay Tree Publishing, 2nd Revised edition May 30, 2006)

- Therapy Gone Mad : The True Story of Hundreds of Patients and a Generation Betrayed Carol Lynn Mithers (Basic Books, 1997)

- Trauma and Recovery Judith Herman, MD (Basic Books, 1997)

94

- The Verbally Abusive Relationship: How to Recognize it and How to Respond Patricia Evans (Adams Media Corporation, 2nd edition 1996)

- Why Does He Do That: Inside the Minds of Angry and Controlling Men Lundy Bancroft (Berkley Publishing Group, 2003)

- Why is it Always About You?: Saving Yourself from the Narcissists in Your Life Sandy Hotchkiss (Free Press, 2002)

Church and State

- American Theocracy : The Peril and Politics of Radical Religion, Oil, and Borrowed Money in the 21st Century Kevin Phillips (Viking Adult, 2006)

- Between Church and State: Religion and Public Education in a Multicultural America James W. Fraser (Palgrave Macmillan September 2, 2000)

- Divided by God: America's Church-State Problem-- and What We Should Do About It Noah Feldman (Farrar, Straus and Giroux June 23, 2005)

- The Founding Fathers and the Place of Religion in America Frank Lambert (Princeton University Press January 9, 2003

- God vs. the Gavel: Religion and the Rule of Law Marci A Hamilton, Edward R. Becker (Cambridge University Press June 17, 2005)

- God's Profits: Faith, Fraud, and the Republican Crusade for Values Voters Sarah Posner (PoliPointPress LLC January 2008)

- The Separation of Church and State: Writings on a Fundamental Freedom by America's Founders Forrest Church (Beacon Press; 1st edition August 9, 2004)

Clergy Abuse

- **A Gospel of Shame: Children, Sexual Abuse and the Catholic Church** Frank Bruni and Elinor Burkett (Perennial, 2002)

- **Tragic Grace: The Catholic Church and Child Sexual Abuse** Stephen J. Rossetti (Liturgical Press, 1996)

- **Betrayal: The Crisis in the Catholic Church** Investigative Staff of the Boston Globe (Bay Back Books, 2003)

- **Pedophiles and Priests: Anatomy of a Contemporary Crisis** Philip Jenkins (Oxford University Press, 2001)

- **Soul Murder God Priest and Me** Sara Atman (Lulu.com March 27, 2007)

Cults

- **Cults: An Educational Volume (DVD)**

- **The Anatomy of Illusion: Religious Cults and Destructive Persuasion** W. Keiser, Jacqueline L. Keiser (Charles C. Thomas Publishing, 1987)

- **Blinded by Deceit** Joanne Hansen (Beaver Pond Press 2002)

- **Bounded Choice: True Believers and Charismatic Cults** Janja Lalich (University of California Press, 2004)

- **Captive Hearts, Captive Minds: Freedom & Recovery from Cults and Abusive Relationships** Janja Lalich (Hunter House Pubs)

- **Charismatic Cult Leaders** Streissguth, Thomas (The Oliver Press Inc, 1995)

- **Corporate Cults: The Insidious Lure of the All-Consuming Organization** Dave Arnott (American Management Association; 1 Ed edition October 1999)

- **Cults and Personality** Frank J. MacHovec (Charles Thomas Publishing, 1989)

96

- Cults: Faith, Healing, and Coercion Marc Galanter (Oxford Univ Press, 1999)

- Cults in our Midst Margaret Singer (Jossey-Bass Publishers, 1995)

- Cults on Campus: Continuing Challenge Marcia Rudin

- "Join Us" (documentary about cults in America) DVD Ondi Timoner

- The Facts About Cults Stevens, Sarah (Crestwood House, 1992)

- From Slogans to Mantras: Social Protest and Religious Conversion in the Late Vietnam Era Stephen Kent and Benjamin Zablocki (Syracuse University Press 2001)

- The Guru Papers: Masks of Authoritarian Power Joel Kramer and Diana Alstad (North Atlantic Books, 1983)

- The Heart of a Cult Lena Phoenix (Garuda, Inc. September 1, 2006)

- Inside Out: A Memoir of Entering and Breaking Out of a Minneapolis Political Cult Alexandra Stein (North Star Press of St. Cloud, 2002)

- Insane Therapy: Portrait of a Psychotherapy Cult Marybeth F. Ayella (Temple Univ Press, 1998)

- Malignant Pied Pipers of Our Time: A Psychological Study of Destructive Cult Leaders from Rev. Jim Jones to Osama bin Laden Peter A. Olsson, M.D. (Publish America, 2005)

- On the Edge: Political Cults of the Left and Right Dennis Tourish and Tim Wohlforth (Sharpe, 2000)

- The Power of Cult Branding Matthew W. Ragas and Bolivar J. Bueno (Prima Publishing, 2002)

- Recovery from Abusive Groups Wendy Ford (American Family Foundation, 1993)

- Recovery From Cults Michael Langone (Editor) (Norton , 1995)

- The Serpent Rising Mary Garden (Hushion House Publishing, 2004)

- Snapping - America's Epidemic of Sudden Personality Change (Second Edition) Flo Conway and Jim Siegelman (Stillpoint Press, 1978, 1995)

- So Late, So Soon, A Memoir D'Arcy Fallon (Hawthorne Books & Literary Arts, LLC 2004)

- Soul Snatchers Jean-Mari Abgrall (Algora Pub., 1999)

- Spiritual Perversion Steve Sanchez (Turnkey Press, February 28, 2005)

- Take Back Your Life: Recovering from Cults and Abusive Relationships Janja Lalich, Madeleine Landau Tobias (Bay Tree Publishing, 2nd Revised edition May 30, 2006)

- The Sullivan Institute/Fourth Wall Community: The Relationship of Radical Individualism and Authoritarianism Amy B. Siskind (Praeger Publishers January 30, 2003)

- Them and Us: Cult Thinking and the Terrorist Threat Arthur J. Deikman and Doris Lessing (Bay Tree Publishing 2003)

- TM and Cult Mania Michael A. Persinger, Normand J. Carrey, Lynn A. Suess (Christopher Pub House, 1980)

- Under the Influence: The Destructive Effects of Group Dynamics John D. Goldhammer (Prometheus Books, 1996)

- The Wrong Way Home: Uncovering the Patterns of Cult Behavior in American Society Arthur J. Deikman, M.D. (Beacon Press, 1994)

Critical Thinking

- In the Name of Love: Abusive Controlling Relationships (DVD)

- Cults: An Educational Volume (DVD)

- A Conscious Life Cox, Fran and Cox, Louis (Conari Press, 1996)

- Amazing Face Reading: An illustrated encyclopedia for reading faces Mac Fulfer (Creative Associates, 1996)

- American Theocracy : The Peril and Politics of Radical Religion, Oil, and Borrowed Money in the 21st Century Kevin Phillips (Viking Adult, 2006)

- Animal Farm George Orwell (Signet Classic, 1996)

- The Art of Happiness: A handbook for living Howard Culter with H.H. Dalai Lama (Riverhead Books, 1998)

- Believed-In Imaginings: The Narrative Construction of Reality Joseph de Rivera and Theodore R. Sarbin (Editors) (American Psychological Assn, 1998)

- The Biology of Belief: How our Biology Biases our Beliefs and Perceptions Joseph Giovannoli (Rosetta Press, 2001)

- Chuck Whitlock's Scam School Charles R. Whitlock and Chuck Whitlock (Hungry Minds October 1997)

- Cognitive Models and Spiritual Maps: Interdisciplinary Explorations of Religious Experience Editors Jensine Andresen, Robert K.C. Forman, Ken Wilber (Imprint Academic, 2001)

- Consciousness Explained Daniel C. Dennett (Little Brown & Co, 1992)

- Craving for Ecstasy Harvey Milkman and Stanley Sunderwirth

- Dark Hero Of The Information Age: In Search of Norbert Wiener, the Father of Cybernetics Flo Conway and Jim Siegelman (Basic Books, 2004)

- Darkness at Noon Arthur Koestler (Vintage UK November 30, 1994)

- The Death of Psychotherapy--From Freud to Alien Abductions Donald A. Eisner (Praeger Publishers Westport, Conn., 2000)

- The Demon-Haunted World: Science as the Candle in the Dark Carl Sagan and Ann Druyan (Ballantine Books, 1997)

- Detecting Lies and Deceit: The Psychology of Lying and Implications for Professional Practice Wiley Series in Psychology of Crime, Policing, and Law By Aldert Vrij (John Wiley and Sons, 2000)

- Encyclopedia of Claims, Frauds and Hoaxes of the Occult and the Supernatural: James Randi's Decidedly Skeptical Definitions of Alternate Realities James Randi (St. Martins Press, 1997)

- Encyclopedia of the Paranormal Gordon Stein, editor Carl Sagan (Prometheus Books, 1996)

- Everybody's Guide to People Watching Aaron Wolfgang (Intercultural Press, 1995)

- Extraordinary Popular Delusions & the Madness of Crowds Charles MacKay and Andrew Tobias (Crown Pub, 1995)

- Faith Beyond Faith Healing: Finding Hope After Shattered Dreams Kimberly Weston (Paraclete Press, 2002)

- Feet of Clay: Saints, Sinners, and Madmen: A Study of Gurus Anthony Storr (Free Press; Reprint edition August 19, 1997)

- The First Honest Book About Lies Joni Kincher (Free Spirit Publishing, 1992)

- Fraud!: How to Protect Yourself from Schemes, Scams, and Swindles Marsha Bertrand (American Management Association; 1 Ed edition October 1999)

- Frauds, Myths and Mysteries Kenneth L. Feder. (Mayfield Publishing, 1998)

- The Fringes of Reason Tim Schultz (editor) (A Whole Earth Catalogue: Harmony Books, 1989).

- From Fetish to God in Ancient Egypt E.A. Wallis Budge (Dover Pub, 1989)

- From Slogans to Mantras: Social Protest and Religious Conversion in the Late Vietnam Era (Religion and Politics)Stephen Kent, PhD (Syracuse University Press, 2001)

- The God Part of the Brain Matthew Alper (Rouge Press, 2001).

- Healing: A Doctor in Search of a Miracle William Nole, M.D. (Random House, 1974)

- How Mumbo-jumbo Conquered the World Francis Wheen (Public Affairs, 2005)

- How the Mind Works Steven Pinker (W.W. Norton & Co, 1999)

- How to Think About Weird Things: Critical Thinking for a New Age Theodore Schick, Jr. and Lewis Vaughn (Mayfield Publishing, 1999)

- Invasion From Mars: A Study in the Psychology of Panic Hadley Cantril (Harper Torchbooks, 1966)

- Karma Cola: Marketing to Mystic East Gita Mehta (Vintage, 1994)

- Leaps of Faith Nicholas Humphrey (Springer; 1 edition June 4, 1999)

- Lies, Lies, Lies! The Psychology of Deceit Charles V. Ford (American Psychiatric Press, 1995)

- The Many Faces of Deceit: Omissions, Lies and Disguise in Psychotherapy Helen K. Gediman and Janice Lieberman (Jason Aronson, 1996)

- Maximize Your Memory Jonathan Hancock (David and Charles, 2000)

- Mind Magic: Tricks for Reading Minds Ormond McGill and Canevari Green (Millbrook Press March 1, 1995)

- Mind Reading and Magic Tricks Bob Longe (Sterling Books, 1999)

- My Father's Guru: A Journey through Spirituality and Disillusion Jeffrey M. Masson (Addision Wesley, 1993)

- The Mystical Mind: Probing the Biology of Religious Experience Andrew Newberg, MD and Eugene G. Aquili, PhD (Fortress Press, 1999)

- The Nazi Doctors: Medical Killing and the Psychology of Genocide Robert Jay Lifton (Basic Books, 2000)

- Nineteen Eighty-four George Orwell (Penguin Books Ltd; New Ed edition January 29, 2004)

- The Observing Self: Mysticism and Psychotherapy Arthur J. Deikman, M.D. (Beacon Press; Reprint edition April 15, 1983)

- Official Know-it-all Guide to Secrets of Mind Power Harry Lorayne (Frederick Fell, 1999)

- On the Wild Side Martin Gardner (Prometheus Books, 1992)

- Physics: Concepts and Connections Art Hobson (Prentice Hall, 2nd edition 1999)

- The Power of Myth Joseph Campbell, Bill Moyers (Contributor), Betty Sue Flowers (Editor) (Anchor, 1991)

- The Practical Dreamer's Handbook: Finding the Time, Money, and Energy to Live the Life You Want to Live Paul and Sarah Edwards (JP Tarcher, 2000)

- Practical Mental Magic Theodore Annemann (Dover, 1983)

- Prophetic Charisma: The Psychology of Revolutionary Religious Personalities Len Oakes (Syracuse Univ. Press, 1997)

- Psychic Mafia M. Lamar Keene, Allen Spraggett, Lamar Keene and V. Raucher (Prometheus Books, 1997)

- The Road to Malpsychia: Humanistic Psychology and Our Discontents Joyce Milton (Encounter Books, 2002)

- The Roots of Evil: The Origins of Genocide and Other Group Violence Ervin Staub (Cambridge University Press, 1992)

- Science and Pseudoscience in Clinical Psychology Steven Jay Lynn (Editor), Scott O. Lilienfeld (Editor), Jeffrey M. Lohr (Editor) (Guilford Press 2002)

- Secrets of Mind Power: How to Organize and Develop the Hidden Powers of Your Mind Harry Lorayne (Frederick Fell, 1999)

- Self-Working Mental Magic: Sixty-Seven Foolproof Mind-Reading Tricks Karl Fulves (Dover, 1989)

- Self-Working Table Magic: Ninety-Seven Foolproof Tricks with Everyday Objects Karl Fulves and Joseph Schmidt (Dover, 1981)

- The Skeptic's Dictionary: A Collection of Strange Beliefs, Amusing Deceptions, and Dangerous Delusions Robert Todd Carroll (John Wiley & Sons, August 2003)

- Telling Lies: Clues to Deceit in the Marketplace, Politics, and Marriage Paul Ekman (W.W. Norton, 2000)

- Trauma and Recovery Judith Herman, MD (Basic Books, 1997)

- Turn Off Your Mind: The Mystic Sixties and the Dark Side of the Age of Aquarius Valentine Lachman (The Disinformation Company 2003)

- The Vanishing Hitchhiker Jan Harold Brunvand (Norton, 1981)

- Weird Water and Fuzzy Logic: More Notes of a Fringe-Watcher Martin Gardner (Prometheus Books, 1996)

- Who's Crazy Anyway Joan Mazza (iUniverse April2000)

- Why God won't go away: Brain Science and the Biology of Belief Andrew Newberg, MD (Ballantine Books, 2001)

- Without Conscience Robert Hare (The Guilford Press January 8, 1999)

- The Wrong Way Home: Uncovering the Patterns of Cult Behaviour in American Society Arthur J. Deikman, M.D. (Beacon Press, 1994)

Destructive Churches

- Amazing Grace Kathleen Norris (Riverhead Books, 1998)

- By What Authority: The Rise of Personality Cults in American Christianity Richard Quebedeaux (Harper Collins, 1981)

- The Changing Face of the Priesthood: A reflection of the Priest's Crisis of Soul Donald B. Cozzens (Liturgical Press, 2000)

- Charismatic Chaos John F. MacArthur, Jr. (Zondervan Publishing House, 1993)

- Churches that Abuse Ronald Enroth (Zondervan Publishing House, 1992)

- Cult Proofing Your Kids Paul Martin (Zondervan Press, 1993)

- Damaged Disciples: Casualties of Authoritarian Churches and the Shepherding Movement Ron and Vicki Burks

- The Drift Into Deception - The Eight Characteristics of Abusive Christianity Agnes C. Lawless with John W. Lawless (Kregel Resources, Grand Rapids, MI, 1995)

- Exposing Spiritual Abuse: How to Rediscover God's Love When the Church Has Let You Down Mike Fehlauer (Charisma House, 2001)

- "Join Us" (documentary about cults in America) DVD Ondi Timoner

- The Grace Awakening Charles Swindoll. (Word Books, 1996)

- Healing Spiritual Abuse : How to Break Free from Bad Church Experiences Ken Blue (InterVarsity Press October 1993)

- The Jesus People; Old-Time Religion in the Age of Aquarius Ronald M. Enroth (Wm. B. Eerdmans Publishing Co., May 1972)

- Lead us not into temptation: Catholic Priests and the Sexual Abuse of Children Berry and Andrew Greely (Univ. of Illinois Press, 2000)

- Letters to a Devastated Christian Gene Edwards (Tyndale House Publishers, Inc, Wheaton, IL 1984, 1992)

- More Jesus, Less Religion: Moving from rules to relationship Stephen Arterburn and Jack Felton (Waterbrook Press, 2000)

- Occult: They Didn't Think it Could Happen in Their Church June Summers (Global Strategic Resources, 2005)

- Sex, Priests and Power: Anatomy of a Crisis A.W. Richard Sipe (Bruner/Mazel, 1995)

- The Subtle Power of Spiritual Abuse - Recognizing and Escaping Spiritual Manipulation and False Spiritual Authority within the Church David Johnson and Jeff VanVonderen (Bethany House Publishers, Mpls. MN, 1991)

- Tithing: Low- Realm, Obsolete & Defunct Matthew E. Narramore (Tedoa Publishing, 2004

- Twisted Scriptures- A Path to Freedom From Abusive Churches Mary Alice Chrnalogar (Control Techniques, Inc. P.O. Box 8021 Chattanooga, TN 37414-8021)

- The Unhealed Wounded: The church and human sexuality Eugene Kennedy (St. Martins Press, 2001)

- Youth, Brainwashing, and the Extremist Cults Ronald M. Enroth (Zondervan Publishing Company November 2000)

Gurus

- The Enlightenment Blues: My years with an American Guru Andre Van Der Braak (Monkfish Book Publishing October 2003)

- Guru Papers: Masks of Authoritarian Power Joel Kramer (Frog, Ltd. May 20, 1993)

- Feet of Clay: Saints, Sinners, and Madmen: A Study of Gurus Anthony Storr (Free Press; Reprint edition August 19, 1997)

- Karma Cola: Marketing to Mystic East Gita Mehta (Vintage, 1994)

- My Life in Orange: Growing up with the Guru Tim Guest (Harvest Books February 1, 2005)

- The 99th Monkey: A Spiritual Journalist's Misadventures with Gurus, Messiahs, Sex, Psychedelics, and Other Consciousness-Raising Experiments Eliezer Sobel (Santa Monica Press February 1, 2008)

106

- The Serpent Rising: A Journey of Spiritual Seduction Mary Garden (Sid Harta Publishers October 2002)

New Age Groups

- A Path With Heart: A Guide Through the Perils and Promises of Spiritual Life Jack Kornfield. (Bantam, 1993)

- Carlos Castaneda, Academic Opportunism and the Psychedelic Sixties Jay Courtney Fikes. (Millinea Press, 1996)

- The New Age: Notes of a Fringe-Watcher Martin Gardner. (Prometheus Books, 1991)

- 19 Years in a New Age Group: Torn from the Arms of Satan Judith L. Carlson, Elizabeth R. Burchard (Ace Academics, 1999)

- Psychic Dictatorship in America Gerald B.Bryan, Talita Paolini, Kenneth Paolini. (Feb 2000)

- Understanding the New Age Russell Chandler. (Zondervan, 1993)

- Lost and Found: My Life in a Group Marriage Commune Margaret Hollenbach (University of New Mexico Press, 2004)

Persuasion Techniques

- In the Name of Love: Abusive Controlling Relationships (DVD)

- Age of Propaganda: The Everyday Use and Abuse of Persuasion Anthony Pratkanis & Elliot Aronson

- Battle for the Mind William Sargent

- Brainwashing: The Science of Thought Control Kathleen Taylor (Oxford University Press August 24, 2006)

- Coercive Persuasion - A Socio-Psychological Analysis of the "Brainwashing" of American Civilian Prisoners by the Chinese Communists Edgar H. Schein with Inge Schneier and Curtis H. Barker (New York WW Norton & Company, 1971)

- Crazy Therapies-What are they? Do they work? Margaret Singer and Janja Lalich (Jossey-Bass, San Francisco 1996)

- Dark Hero Of The Information Age: In Search of Norbert Wiener, the Father of Cybernetics Flo Conway and Jim Siegelman (Basic Books, 2004)

- Easily Fooled: New Insights and Techniques for Resisting Manipulation Bob Fellows (Mind Matters, 2000)

- Easily Led: A History of Propaganda Oliver Tomson (Sutton Press, 1999)

- From Slogans to Mantras: Social Protest and Religious Conversion in the Late Vietnam Era Stephen A. Kent (Syracuse University Press, 2001)

- Get Anyone to Do Anything and Never Feel Powerless Again : Psychological Secrets to Predict, Control, and Influence Every Situation David J. Lieberman (St. Martin's Press; 1st edition May 10, 2000)

- The Hidden Persuaders Vance Packard (Pocket; Updated edition June 3, 1984)

- Hypnotism Investigated Tony Bamgridge. (Renew February 1998)

- Influence Robert B. Cialdini, Ph.D. (Quill, NY, 1984 (Revised 1993))

- The Manipulated Mind: Brainwashing, Conditioning, and Indoctrination Denise Winn (Malor Books, 2000)

- Obedience to Authority Stanley Milgram (Harper Perennial August 8, 1983)

- People Who Play God: How Ultra-Authorities Enslave the Hearts, Minds, Souls of Their Victims Beth E. Peterson (Xlibris Corp., 2003)

- Ponzi Schemes, Invaders from Mars and More Extraordinary Popular Delusions and the Madness of Crowds Joseph Bulgatz (Harmony Books)

- The Power of Cult Branding: How 9 Magnetic Brands Turned Customers Into Loyal Followers (and Yours Can, Too)Matthew W. Ragas, Bolivar J. Bueno (Prima Publishing, 2002)

- The Psychology of Attitude Change and Social Influence Philip Zimbardo (McGraw-Hill Humanities/Social Sciences/Languages; 3 edition February 1, 1991)

- Rape of the MindJ.Meerloo (Putnam Pub Group, 2000)

- Stages of Faith - The Psychology of Human Development and the Quest for Meaning James W. Fowler (Harper Collins, 1995)

- The True Believer Eric Hoffer (Harper and Row, 1951)

- Thought Reform and the Psychology of Totalism - A Study of Brainwashing in ChinaRobert J. Lifton, MD. (The University of N.C. Press Original Publisher: Norton and Co., 1961)

- Under the Influence: The Destructive Effects of Group Dynamics John D. Goldhammer (Prometheus Books, 1996)

- When Prophecy Fails Leon Festinger, Henry W. Riecken and Stanley Schachter (Harpercollins College Div June 1964)

Repressed Memories & MPD

- The Best Kept Secret: Sexual Abuse of Children Florence Rush. (Prentice Hall Trade October 1980)

- Child Sexual Abuse and False Memory Syndrome Robert A. Baker (Editor). (Prometheus Books, 1998

- The Cognitive Neuropsychology of False Memories: A Special Issue of Cognitive Neuropsychology Daniel L. Schacter (Editor). (Taylor & Francis, 1999)

- Confabulations: Creating False Memories, Destroying Families Eleanor C. Goldstein, Kevin Farmer (Editor) (Social Issues Resources Series, 1992)

- Crazy Therapies Margaret Thaler Singer, Janja Lalich (Contributor) (Jossey-Bass, 1996)

- Creating Hysteria: Women and Multiple Personality Disorder Joan Ross Acocella (Jossey-Bass, 1999)

- Diagnosis for Disaster: The Devastating Truth About False Memory Syndrome and Its Impact on Accusers and Families Claudette Wassil-Grimm (Penquin USA, 1996)

- Eyewitness Testimony Elizabeth F. Loftus (Harvard University Press, 1996)

- False-Memory Creation in Children and Adults: Theory, Research, and Implications David F. Bjorklund (Editor). (Lawrence Erlbaum Assoc, 2000)

- How We Know What Isn't So: The Fallibility of Human Reason in Everyday Life Thomas Gilovich (Free Press, 1993)

- Making Monsters: False Memories, Psychotherapy and Sexual Hysteria Richard Ofshe and Ethan Watters (Charles Scribner's Sons NY, 1994)

- Manufacturing Victims: What the Psychology Industry Is Doing to People Tana Dineen (Robert Davies Publishers, 1998)

- Memory Distortion: How Minds, Brains, and Societies Reconstruct the Past Daniel L. Schacter (Editor). (Harvard University Press, 1997)

- The Myth of Repressed Memory: False Memories and Allegations of Sexual Abuse Elizabeth Loftus, Katherine Ketcham (St. Martin's Press, 1996)

- National Incidence Studies on Missing, Abducted, Runaway, and Thrownaway Children in America David Finkelhor (DIANE Publishing, 1990)

- Psychology Astray: Fallacies in Studies of 'Repressed Memory' and Childhood Trauma Harrison G Pope, Jr., MD (Social Issues Resources Series, 1997)

- Recovered Memories of Child Sexual Abuse: Psychological, Social, and Legal Perspectives on a Contemporary Mental Health Controversy Sheila Taub (Editor). (Charles C. Thomas Publishers, 1999)

- 'Recovered Memory' and Other Assaults upon the Mysteries of Consciousness: Hypnosis, Psychotherapy, Fraud and the Mass Media William Rogers (McFarland and Company, 1995)

- Science of False Memory, The Charles J. Brainerd, Valerie J. Reyna (Oxford University Press, 2005)

- Second Thoughts Paul Simpson (Thomas Nelson, 1997)

- Searching for Memory: The Brain, The Mind, and The Past Daniel L. Schacter (Editor). (Harper Collins, 1997)

- Slaughter of Innocents: Child abuse through the ages and today Sander J. Breiner. (Plenum Pr April 1990)

- Suggestions of Abuse: True and False Memories of Childhood Michael D. Yapdo, Ph.D (Diane Books Publishing Company April 1994)

- Survivor Psychology: The Dark Side of a Mental Health Mission Susan Smith (Social Issues Resources Series, 1998)

- Therapy Gone Mad : The True Story of Hundreds of Patients and a Generation Betrayed Carol Lynn Mithers (Basic Books, 1997)

- Therapy's Delusions: The Myth of the Unconscious and the Exploitation of Today's Walking Worried Ethan Watters and Richard Ofshe (Simon & Schuster, 1999)

- Too Scared to Cry: Psychic Trauma in Childhood Lenore Terr (Harper Collins, 1992)

- Trance on Trial Alan W. Scheflin, LL.M. and Jerold Lee Shaprio, Ph.D (The Guilford Press August 4, 1989)

- Truth in Memory Steven J. Lynn (Editor), Kevin M. McConkey (Editor) (Guilford Press, 1998)

- Victims of Memory - Incest Accusations and Shattered Lives Mark Pendergrast (Upper Access Inc. VT, 1995)

- Wounded Innocents: The Real Victims of the War Against Child Abuse Richard Wexler (Prometheus Books, 1995)

Terrorists and Terrorism

- American Jihad: The Terrorists Living Amongst Us Steven Emerson (Simon and Schuster, 2002)

- American Terrorist: Timothy McVeigh and the Oklahoma City Bombing Lou Michel, Dan Harbeck (Regan Books, 2001)

- Eco-Terrorism & Eco-Extremism Against Agriculture Joseph M. Miller and R.M. Miller (Joseph a Miller - R M Miller; Spiral edition January 5, 2000)

- Holy War Inc.: Inside the Secret World of Osama bin Laden Peter Bergen (Free Press, 2001)

- Inside Terrorism Bruce Hoffman. (Columbia University Press, 1999)

- The Militia Threat: Terrorists Among Us Robert L. Snow (Perseus Press, 1999)

- The New Jackals: Ramzi Youseff, Osama bin Laden and the Future of Terrorism Simon Reeve (Northeastern University Press, 1999)

- The New Terrorism: Fanaticism and the Arms of Mass Destruction Walter Laqueur (Oxford University Press, 1999)

- Origins of Terrorism: Psychologies, Ideologies, Theologies, States of Mind Walter Reich (Woodrow Wilson Center Press, 1998)

- Profiles in Terrorism: Twenty Years of Anti-Abortion Terrorism Frederick Clarkson (Common Courage Press, 2000)

- Targets of Hatred: Anti-Abortion Terrorism Patricia Baird-Windle, Eleanor J. Bader (Palgrave Macmillan, 2001)

- Terror in the Mind of God: The Global Rise of Religious Violence Mark Jeurgensmeyer. (University of California Press, 2001)

- Them and US: Cult Thinking and the Terrorist Threat Arthur Deikman (Bay Tree Publishing September 25, 2003)

- Usama bin Laden's Al-Qaida: Profile of a Terrorist Network Yonah Alexander and Michael S. Setnam (Transnational Publishing, 2001)

Groups of Interest

Al-Qaeda, Osama bin Laden

- Holy War Inc.: Inside the Secret World of Osama bin Laden Peter Bergen (Free Press, 2001)

- The New Jackals: Ramzi Youseff, Osama bin Laden and the Future of Terrorism Simon Reeve (Northeastern University Press, 1999)

- Usama bin Laden's al-Qaida: Profile of a Terrorist Network Yonah Alexander and Michael S. Setnam (Transnational Publishing, 2001)

Amish

- Crossing Over: One Woman's Escape from Amish Life Ruth Irene Garrett and Rick Farrant (Harper San Francisco, January 7, 2003)

Amway

- Amway Motivational Organizations: Behind the Smoke and Mirrors Ruth Carter (Backstreet Publishing September 1, 1999)

- Amway: The Cult of Free Enterprise Stephen Butterfield (South End Press, 1985)

Aum Shinrikyo

- Aum Shinrikyo -- Japan's Unholy Sect Rei Kimura (GreatUnpublished.com, 2002)

- The Cult at the End of the World: The Terrifying Story of the Aum Doomsday Cult, From the Subways of Tokyo to Arsenals in Russia David E. Kaplan and Andrew Marshall (Crown Publishing, 1996)

- Destroying the World to Save It: Aum Shinrikyo, Apocalyptic Violence, and the New Global Terrorism Robert Jay Lifton (Owl Books September 1, 2000)

- Holy Terror: Armageddon in Tokyo D.W. Brackett (Weatherhill, 1996)

Bhagwan Shree Rajneesh

- My Life in Orange: Growing up with the Guru Tim Guest (Harvest Books February 1, 2005)

Robin Jackson

The Brethren

- From Dean's List to Dumpsters Jim Guerra (Dorrance Publishing Company, 2000)

Catholic Sects

- More Catholic than The Pope: And Inside Look At Traditionalism
  Patrick Madrid, Pete Vere (Our Sunday Visitor September 30, 2004)

- The Pope's Armada : Unlocking the Secrets of Mysterious and Powerful New Sects in the Church
  Gordon Urquhart (Prometheus Books, 1999)

- Smoke of Satan: Conservative and Traditionalist Dissent in Contemporary Catholicism Michael W. Cuneo (John Hopkins University Press, 1999)

- Vows of Silence: The Abuse of Power in the Papacy of John Paul II
  Jason Berry and Gerald Renner (Free Press, 2004)

Children of God/The Family

- Blinded by Deceit Joanne Hansen (Beaver's Pond Press, 2002)

- Heaven's Harlots: My Fifteen Years as a Sacred Prostitute in the Children of God Cult Miriam Williams (William Morrow, 1998)

- Jesus Freaks: A True Story of Murder and Madness on the Evangelical Edge Don Lattin HarperOne (October 9, 2007)

- Not Without My Sister Christina Jones, Celeste Jones, Juliana Burhring (HarperCollins Entertainment July 2, 2007)

Christian Fundamentalists

- Behind the Scenes: The True Face of Fake Faith Healers Yves A. Brault (FirstPublish, 2000)

115

- The Dark Side: How Evangelical Teachings Corrupt Love and Truth Valerie Tarico, Ph.D. (Lulu.com Paperback -- January 18, 2007)

- Divine Destruction: Dominion Theology and American Environmental Policy Stephenie Hendricks (Melville House 2005)

- Eternal Hostility--The Struggle Between Theocracy and Democracy Frederick Clarkson (Common Courage Press, 1997)

- Faith Beyond Faith Healing: Finding Hope After Shattered Dreams Kimberly Weston (Paraclete Press, 2002)

- From Rapture to Revelation: Addressing the Spiritual and Theological Concerns of Former Fundamentalists in the United States of America Michelle Grace Lyerly (Wolf & Stock Publishers August 2006)

- The Fundamentals of Extremism Kimberly Blaker (New Boston Books, 2003)

- Holy Terror - The Fundamentalist War on America's Freedoms and Religion Politics in our private lives Flo Conway and Jim Siegelman (Delta Books, Del Publishing, 1982)

- The Jew and the Christian Missionary: A Jewish Response to Missionary Christianity Gerald Sigal (KTAV Publishing, 1981)

- The Jew and the Christian Missionary: A Jewish Response to Missionary Christianity Gerald Sigal (KTAV Publishing, 1981)

- Kingdom Coming: The Rise of Christian Nationalism Michelle Goldberg (W. W. Norton May 11, 2006)

- The Mind of the Bible-Believer Edmund Cohen (Prometheus Books, 1988)

- The Rapture Exposed: The Message of Hope in the Book of Revelation Barbara R. Rossing (Westview Press, 2004)

- Rescuing the Bible from Fundamentalism John Shelby Spong (Harper Collins, 1992)

- Spiritual Warfare: The Politics of the Christian Right Sara Diamond (South End Press, 1989)

- Stealing Jesus : How Fundamentalism Betrays Christianity Bruce Bawer (Three Rivers Press, 1998)

- Thy Kingdom Come: How the Religious Right Distorts the Faith and Threatens America: An Evangelical's Lament Randall Balmer (Perseus Books Group July 31, 2006)

- Why the Religious Right is Wrong: About Separation of Church and State Rob Boston, Robert Boston and Barry W. Lynn (Prometheus Books, 1994)

Christian Science

- Faith Beyond Faith Healing: Finding Hope After Shattered Dreams Kimberly Weston (Paraclete Press, 2002)

- God's Perfect Child: Living and Dying in the Christian Science Church Caroline Fraser (Owl Books 2000)

- The Healing Revelations of Mary Baker Eddy: The Rise and Fall of Christian Science Martin Gardener (Prometheus Books, 1993)

- The Religion That Kills - Christian Science: Abuse, Neglect, and Mind Control Dr. Linda S. Kramer (Huntington House Publishers)

Chung Moo Quan (later Chung Moo Doe and now called Oom Yung)

- Herding the Moo: Exploits of a Martial Arts Cult Joe Smith (Trafford Publishing May 4, 2006)

Andrew Cohen and Moksha Foundation

- Enlightenment Blues: My years with an American Guru Andre van der Braak (Consortium Book Sales & Dist 2003)

- The Mother of God Luna Tarlo

The Endeavour Academy--Chuck Anderson, a.k.a. "The Master Teacher"

- Complete Story of the Course : The History, the People, and the Controversies Behind a Course in Miracles D. Patrick Miller, (Fearless Books, August 1997)

Extremists and Hate Groups

- A Force Upon the Plain - The American Militia Movement and the Politics of Hate Kenneth S. Stern (Simon and Schuster, NY 1996)

- American Extremists: Militias, Supremacists, Klansmen, Communists and Others John George and Laird Wilcox (Prometheus Books, 1996)

- American Terrorist: Timothy McVeigh and the Oklahoma City Bombing Lou Michel, Dan Harbeck (Regan Books, 2001)

- Animal Rights: History and Scope of a Radical Social Movement Harold D. Guither (Southern Illinois Univ. Press, 1998)

- The Bondage of Self Kirsten Helene Kaiser (Milo House Press August 15, 2002)

- Conspiracy Theories: Secrecy and Power in American Culture Mark Fenster (University of Minnesota Press, 1999)

- Documents of American Prejudice: An Anthology of Writings on Race from Thomas Jefferson to David Duke S.T. Joshi (Basic Books, 1999)

118

- Dragons of God: A Journey Through Far Right America Vincent Coppola (Longstreet Press, 1997)

- Eco-Terrorism & Eco-Extremism Against Agriculture Joseph M. Miller and R.M. Miller (Joseph a Miller - R M Miller; Spiral edition January 5, 2000)

- Encyclopedia of White power: A Sourcebook on the Radical Racist Right Jeffrey Kaplan (Altamira Pass, 2000)

- Enemies Within: The Culture of Conspiracy in Modern America Robert Alan Goldberg (Yale University Press, 2001)

- The Fiery Cross: The Ku Klux Klan in America Craig Wade (Oxford University Press, 1998)

- From Slogans to Mantras: Social Protest and Religious Conversion in the Late Vietnam Era Stephen A. Kent (Syracuse University Press, 2001)

- Gathering Storm: America's Militia Threat James Corcoran (Harper Perennial April 23, 1997)

- Hooded Americanism: The History of the Ku Klux Klan David Mark Chalmers (Duke University Press, 1987)

- In God's Country: The Patriot Movement and the Pacific Northwest David A. Neiwert (Washington State University Press, 1999)

- Inside Organized Racism: Women in the Hate Movement Kathleen M. Blee (University of California Press, 2002)

- Live from the Gates of Hell: An Insider's Look at the Anti-Abortion Movement Jerry Reiter (Prometheus Books, 2000)

- The Militia Threat: Terrorists Among Us Robert L. Snow (Perseus Press, 1999)

- One Aryan Nation Under God: How Religious Extremists Use the Bible to Justify Their Actions Jerome Walters (Sourcebooks, 2001)

- Origins of Terrorism: Psychologies, Ideologies, Theologies, States of Mind Walter Reich (Woodrow Wilson Center Press, 1998)

- The Politics of the Extreme Right: From the Margins to the Mainstream Paul Hainsworth (London: Pinter, 2000)

- The Politics of Unreason Seymour M. Lipset and Earl Raab (Harper & Bro Place of Publication, 1978)

- Profiles in Terrorism: Twenty Years of Anti-Abortion Terrorism Frederick Clarkson (Common Courage Press, 2000)

- The Racist Mind: Portraits of American Neo-Nazis and Klansmen Raphael S. Ezekiel (Penguin US, 1996)

- Religion and the Racist Right: The Origins of the Christian Identity Movement Michael Barkun (University of North Carolina Press, 1996)

- Selling Fear: Conspiracy Theories and End Times Paranoia Gregory S. Camp (Baker Pub Group March 1997)

- Soldiers of God: White Supremacists and their Holy War for America Howard Bushart (Pinnacle Books, 1999)

- Suburban Warriors: The Origins of the New American Right Lisa McGirr (Princeton University Press, 2001)

- Tabernacle of Hate: Why They Bombed Oklahoma City Kerry Noble (Voyageur Pub, 1998)

- Targets of Hatred: Anti-Abortion Terrorism Patricia Baird-Windle, Eleanor J. Bader (Palgrave Macmillan, 2001)

- Terror in the Mind of God: The Global Rise of Religious Violence Mark Jeurgensmeyer. (University of California Press, 2001)

- The Terrorist Next Door: The Militia Movement and the Radical Right Daniel Levitas (St. Martin's Griffin, January 2004)

- The War Against the Greens: The "Wise Use" Movement, The New Right and Anti-Environmental Violence David Helvarg (Sierra Club Books, 1997)

- Waves of Rancor: Tuning in the Radical Right (Media, Communication, and Culture in America) Robert L. Hilliard, Michael C. Keith and Donald Fishman (Published by M.E. Sharpe, 1999)

- The White Separatist Movement in the United States: White Power, White Pride Betty A. Dobratz, Stephanie L. Shanks-Meile (John Hopkins University Press, 2000)

Gothard, Bill

- A Matter of Basic Principles: Bill Gothard and the Christian Life Don Veinot (Midwest Christian Outreach August 25, 2003)Order

Heaven's Gate

- Cosmic Suicide: The Tragedy and Transcendence of Heaven's Gate Forrest Jackson, Rodney Perkins (Pentaradial Press, 1997)

- The Keepers of Heaven's Gate: The Millennial Madness, the Religion Behind the Rancho Santa Fe Suicides William Henry, Cary Anderson (Earthpulse Press, 1997)

Benny Hinn

- Behind the Scenes: The True Face of Fake Faith Healers Yves A. Brault (FirstPublish, 2000)

- The Confusing World of Benny Hinn G. Richard Fisher and M. Kurt Goedelman (Personal Freedom Outreach, 1997)

International Church of Christ

- Bewitchment: You Foolish Galatians Timothy Williams (WinePress Publishing, 2002)

Islamic Fundamentalism

- Taliban: Militant Islam, Oil and Fundamentalism in Central Asia Ahmed Rashid (Yale University Press, 2001)

- Triumph of Disorder: Islamic Fundamentalism, The New Face of War Morgan Norval (McKenna Publishing, 2001)

Jehovah's Witnesses

- 30 Years a Watchtower Slave: The Confessions of a Converted Jehovah's Witness William J. Schell (Baker Books; Abridged edition December 2001)

- Answering Jehovah's Witnesses: Subject by Subject David A. Reed (Baker Books April 1996)

- Apocalypse Delayed: The Story of Jehovah's Witnesses M. James Penton (University of Toronto Press; 2nd edition March 1998)

- Awakening of a Jehovah's Witness: Escape from the Watchtower Society Dianne Wilson (Prometheus Books, 2002)

- Blood on the Altar: Confessions of a Jehovah's Witness Minister David A. Reed (Prometheus Books, 1996)

- Captives of a Concept (Anatomy of an Illusion) Don Cameron (Lulu Press, 2005)

- Crisis of Conscience Raymond Franz, former member of the Governing Body of Jehovah's Witnesses (Commentary Press, Atlanta, 1983)

- The Four Presidents of the Watch Tower Society Jehovah's Witnesses Edmund C. Gruss (Xulon Press December 2003)

- The Gentile Times Reconsidered: Chronology & Christ's Return Carl O. Jonsson (Commentary Press; 3rd edition July 1998)

- Have You Seen My Mother Jerry Bergman, Bryan Lee McGlothin (Taurleo Publishing , 2005)

- In Search of Christian Freedom Raymond Franz (Commentary Press, 1992)

- Jehovah's Witnesses and the Third Reich: Sectarian Politics under Persecution M. James Penton (University of Toronto Press November 27, 2004)

- Jehovah's Witnesses-- their monuments to false prophecy Edumund C. Gruss (Witness Inc 1997)

- Losing The Faith: Truth under Scrutiny Robin Jackson (Jacko Consulting/Lulu Press)

- The Orwellian World of Jehovah's Witnesses Heather Botting, Gary Botting (University of Toronto Press May 1, 1984)

- Out of the Cocoon: a Young Woman's Courageous Flight from the Grip of a Religious Cult Brenda Lee (Robert D. Reed Publishers, 2006)

- The Sign of the Last Days Carl Olof Jonsson and Wolfgang Herbst (Commentary Pr September 1987)

- The Truth Book: Escaping a Childhood of Abuse Among Jehovah's Witnesses Joy Castro (Aracade Publishing, 2005)

- Understanding Jehovah's Witnesses Robert M. Bowman, Jr.(Baker Book House, 1991)

"Jews for Jesus"

- Hawking God - A Young Jewish Woman's Ordeal in Jews for Jesus Ellen Kamentsky (Sapphire Press)

- Jesus and Judaism E.P. Sanders (Fortress Press, 1987)

- The Jew and the Christian Missionary: A Jewish Response to Missionary Christianity Gerald Sigal (KTAV Publishing, 1981)

- Judaism and Christianity: The Differences Trude Weiss-Rosmarin (Jonathan David Pub., 1997)

- What do Jews Believe: The Spiritual Foundations of Judaism David S. Ariel (Schocken Books, 1996)

Jonestown/ Jim Jones and the Peoples Temple

- The Children of Jonestown Kenneth Wooden (McGraw Hill)

- The Cult that Died: The Tragedy of Jim Jones and the People's Temple George Klineman (Putnam 1980)

- The Ghosts of November: Memoirs of an Outsider Who Witnessed the Carnage at Jonestown, Guyana Jeffrey Brailey (J&J Publishers, 1998)

- Raven: The untold story of the Rev. Jim Jones and His People Tim Reiterman, John Jacobs (Planeta Pub Corp., 1986)

- Seductive Poison Deborah Layton (Anchor Books, 1998)

- Six Years with God: Life Inside Jim Jones' People's Temple Jeannie Mills (A&W, 1979)

- Suicide Cult: The Inside Story of the Peoples Temple Sect and the Massacre in Guyana Marshall Kilduff and Ron Javers (Bantam Books, 1978)

- White Night: The True story of what happened before and after Jonestown John Peer Nugent (Scribner, 1979)

Krishna

- Betrayal of the Spirit Nori Muster (University of Illinois Press November 1996)

- Devotee Farm George Vaishnava (Upfront Publishing, 2002)

- Monkey on a Stick John Hubner and Lindsey Gruson (Onyx Books; Reprint edition March 1990)

- Servant of the Lotus Feet: A Hare Krishna Odyssey Gabriel Brandis (Universe Inc., 2004)

Landmark Education/EST, the Forum

- Outrageous Betrayal : The Real Story of Werner Erhard from Est to Exile Steven Pressman (St Martins Pr; 1st edition August 1993)

- Werner Erhard: The Transformation of a Man. The Founding of EST W.W. Bartley, III. (Clarkson N. Potter, Inc, 1978)

Lyndon Larouche

- Lyndon Larouche and the New American Fascism Dennis King (Doubleday; 1st ed edition January 1, 1989)

Charles Manson

- Helter Skelter: The True Story of the Manson Murders Vincent Bugliosi, Curt Gentry (Bantam Books, 1996)

- The Long Prison Journey of Leslie Van Houten: Life Beyond the Cult Karlene Faith (Northeastern University Press, 2001)

- Manson: The Unholy Trail of Charlie and the Family John Gilmore, Ron Kenner (Amok Books, 2000)

- Manson in His Own Words Charles Manson, Nuel Emmons
  (Grove Press, 1998)

The Mormon Church/The Church of Jesus Christ
of the Latter Day Saints--LDS

- American Massacre: The Tragedy at Mountain
  Meadows Sally Denton (Knopf, 2003)

- Early Mormonism and the Magic World View D.
  Michael Quinn (Signature Books, 1998)

- Inside the Mind of Joseph Smith : Psychobiography
  and the Book of Mormon Robert D. Anderson (Signature
  Books, 1999)

- Inside Today's Mormonism: Understanding Latter-
  day Saints in Light of Biblical Truth Richard Abanes
  (Harvest House Publishers January 1, 2007)

- Leaving the Fold: Candid Conversations with
  Inactive Mormons James W. Ure (Signature Books, 1999)

- Leaving the Saints Martha Beck

- Losing a Lost Tribe: Native Americans, DNA, and
  the Mormon Church Simon G. Southerton (Signature Books,
  2004)

- Mormon America: The Power and the Promise
  Richard N. Ostling, Joan K. Ostling (Harper, 2000)

- The Mormon Conspiracy Charles L. Wood (Black Forest
  Book Promotions, 2001)

- The Mormon Hierarchy: Extensions of PowerD.
  Michael Quinn (Signature Books, 1997)

- The Mormon Murders: A True Story of Greed,
  Forgery, Deceit and Death Steven Naifeh (Onyx Books,
  Reissue edition 1989)

- Mormon Polygamy - A History Richard S. Van Wagoner
  (Signature Books, 1986 (Salt Lake City, UT)

126

- The Mysteries of Godliness: A History of Mormon Temple Worship David John Buerger (Signature Books, 1994)

- No Man Knows My History-The Life of Joseph Smith Fawn M. Brodie (Alfred A. Knopf, Inc., 1971)

- The Pattern of the Double-Bind in Mormonism Marion Stricker (Universal Publishers, 2000)

- Quest for the Gold Plates: Thomas Stuart Ferguson's Archaeological Search for the Book of Mormon Stan Larson (Freethinker Press, 1998)

- Reconsidering No Man Knows My History : Fawn M. Brodie and Joseph Smith in Retrospect Newell G. Bringhurst (Utah State University Press August 1996)

- Secret Ceremonies: A Mormon Woman's Intimate Diary of Marriage and Beyond Deborah Laake (William Morrow and Company, 1993)

- Studies of the Book of Mormon Brigham D. Madsen (Editor), B. H. Roberts, Sterling M. McMurrin (September 1992)

Multi-Level Marketing

- All that Glitters is not God: Breaking Free From the Sweet Deceit of Multi-Level Marketing Athena Dean (Wine Press Publishing, 1998)

- Consumed by Success: Reaching the Top and Finding God wasn't there Athena Dean (Wine Press Publishing, 1997)

- False Profits: Financial and Spiritual Deliverance in Multi-Level Marketing and Pyramid Schemes Robert Fitzpatrick and Joyce K. Reynolds (Herald Press, 1997)

- Home Businesses You can Buy: The Definitive Guide to Exploring Franchises, Multi-Level Marketing and Business Opportunities Paul and Sarah Edwards (Walter Zooi, JP Tarcher, 1997)

- Spellbound: My Journey Through a Tangled Web of Success Robert Morgan Styler (Sandy Creek Publishing; 1 edition January 1, 1998)

- You Can't Cheat an Honest Man: How Ponzi Schemes and Pyramid Frauds Work...and Why They're More Common Than Ever James Walsh (Silver Lake) (Merritt Publishing 1998)

Nation of Islam

- Inside the Nation of Islam, A Historical and Personal Testimony by a Black Muslim Vibert White (University Press of Florida, 2001)

Nuwaubians

- Ungodly: A True Story of Unprecedented Evil Bill Osinski (Indigo Custom Publishing May 2007)

Oneness Pentecostalism

- Christianity Without the Cross: A History of Salvation in Oneness Pentecostalism Thomas A. Fudge (Universal Publishers, 2003)

Opus Dei

- Beyond the Threshold: A Life in Opus Dei Maria del Carmen Tapia (Continuum Pub Group, 1998)

- Opus Dei: An Objective Look Behind the Myths and Reality of the most Controversial Force in the Catholic Church John L. Allen Jr. (Doubleday Religion 2005)

- Opus Dei: An Investigation into the Powerful Secretive Society within the Catholic Church Michael Walsh Harper (San Francisco 2004)

- The Popes Armada: Unlocking the Secrets of Mysterious and Powerful New Sects in the Church Gordon Urquhart (Transworld Publishers Limited, May 1996)

- Saints and Schemers: Opus Dei and Its Paradoxes
  Juan Estruch, Joan Estruch, Elizabeth L. Glick (American
  Philological Association, September 1995)

- Their Kingdom Come: Inside the Secret World of
  Opus Dei Robert A. Hutchison (St. Martin's Press, June 1999)

Polygamists

- Colorado City Polygamists: An Inside Look for the
  Outsider Benjamin G. Bistline (Agreka Books; 1 edition July 21,
  2004)

- Daughter of the Saints: Growing up in Polygamy
  Dorothy Allred Solomon (W.W. Northon & Company, 2004)

- Escape Carolyn Jessop, Laura Palmer (Hardcover - Oct 16, 2007)

- God's Brothel: The Extortion of Sex for Salvation in
  Contemporary Mormon and Christian
  Fundamentalist Polygamy Andrea Moore Emmett (Prince-
  Nez Press, 2004)

- His Favourite Wife Susan Ray Schmidt (Paperback - Jun 15,
  2006)

- Inside the World of Warren Jeffs Carole A., Dr. Western
  (Wyndham House Publishing November 15, 2007)

- Mormon Polygamy: A History Richard S. Van Wagoner
  (Signature Books 1992)

- The Polygamists: A History of Colorado City,
  Arizona Benjamin G. Bistline (Agreka Books, 2004)

- Polygamous Families in Contemporary Society
  Sterling M. McMurrin, Irwin Altman, Joseph Ginat (Cambridge
  University Press 1996)

- Predators, Prey, and Other Kinfolk: Growing Up in
  Polygamy Dorothy Allred Solomon (W.W. Norton & Company
  2003)

- The Secret Lives of Saints: Child Brides and Lost Boys in a Polygamous Mormon Sect Daphne Bramham (Random House Canada March 25, 2008)

- The Secret Story of Polygamy Kathleen Tracy (Sourcebooks 2001)

- Shattered Dreams: My Life as a Polygamist's Wife Irene Spencer (Center Street August 22, 2007)

- Sister Wife Natalie R. Collins (Zumaya Publications, 2003)

- The Sixth of Seven Wives: Escape from Modern Day Polygamy Mary Mckert (Truth Publishing, 2000)

- A Teenager's Tears : When Parents Convert to Polygamy John R. Llewellyn (Agreka Books 2001)

- When Men Become Gods: Mormon Polygamist Warren Jeffs, His Cult of Fear, and the Women Who Fought Back Stephen Singular (St. Martin's Press April 21, 2008)

- Wives and Sisters Nalie R. Collins (St. Martin's Press, 2004)

Sai Baba

- Avatar of Night: The Millennial Edition Tal Brooke (End Run Publishing, 1999)

Sahaja Yoga

- Sahaja Yoga Dr Judith Coney (Curzon Press, 2000)

- Shamans, Mystics and Doctors Dr Sudhir Kakar (University Of Chicago Press; Reprint edition April 9, 1991)

- The Shortest Journey Philippa Pullar (Unwin Paperbacks, 1984)

Satanism

- A City Possessed: The Christchurch Civic Crèche Case Lynley Hood (Longacre Press, 2001)

- The Day Care Ritual Abuse Moral Panic Mary de Young (McFarland and Company 2004)

- In Pursuit of Satan: The Police and the Occult Robert D. Hicks (Prometheus Books, 1991)

- Raising the Devil: Satanism, New Religions and the Media Bill Ellis (University Press of Kentucky 2000)

- Satan's Silence: Ritual Abuse and the Making of a Modern American Witch Hunt Debbie Nathan and Michael Snedeker (Basic Books, 1995)

Scientology

- A Piece of Blue Sky - Scientology, Dianetics, and L. Ron Hubbard Exposed Jon Atack (NY Carol, 1990)

- Bare Faced Messiah - The True Story of L. Ron Hubbard Russell Miller (M. Joseph 1987)

- L. Ron Hubbard - Messiah or Madman? Bent Corydon (Fort Lee, NJ Barricade Books, 1992)

Seventh Day Adventist

- The White Lie Walter Rea (M&R Publications, 1982)

Synanon

- The Light On Synanon : How A Country Weekly Exposed A Corporate Cult-And Won The Pulitzer Prize Dave Mitchell (The Point Reyes Light, 1979)

Transcendental Meditation

- TM and Cult Mania Michael A. Persinger, Normand J. Carrey and Lynn A. Suess (Christopher Pub House, 1980)

- The Maharishi Effect: A Personal Journey Through the Movement That Transformed American Spirituality Geoff Gilpin (Tarcher October 19, 2006)

Trinity Foundation - Ole Anthony

- I Can't Hear God Any More: Life in a Dallas Cult Wendy J. Duncan (VM Life Resources 2006)

Ultra Orthodox Jewish Groups

- The Faith of the Mithnagdim: The Rabbinic Responses to Hasidic Rapture Allan Nadler (Johns Hopkins Jewish Studies, 1997)

- The Rebbe, the Messiah, and the Scandal of Orthodox Indifference David Berger (Littman Library of Jewish Civilization, September 2001)

- Rescued from the Reich: How One of Hitler's Soldiers Saved the Lubavitcher Rebbe Mark Rigg (Yale University Press, 2004)

Unification Church/Rev. Moon

- Bad Moon Rising John Gorenfeld (Polipoint Press March 1, 2008)

- Heartbreak and Rage: Ten years under Sung Myung Moon Gordon Neufeld (Virtual Bookwork, 2002)

- Hostage to Heaven: Four Years in the Unification Cult Barbara Underwood, Betty Underwood (Random House Value Publishing December 12, 1988)

- In the Shadow of the Moons: My Life in the Reverend Sun Myung Moon's Family Nansook Hong (Little Brown & Company, 1998)

Urantia

- Urantia: The Great Cult Mystery Martin Gardner (Prometheus Books, 1995)

Waco Davidians/David Koresh

- See No Evil: Blind Devotion and Blood Shed in David Koresh's Holy War Tim Madigan (The Summit Group, Fort Worth TX, 1993)

- Mad Man In Waco: The Complete Story of the Davidian Cult, David Koresh and the Waco Massacre Brad Bailey & Bob Darden (WRS Publishers, 1993)

- Inside the Cult Marc Breault & Martin King (Signet Books, 1993)

- Massacre at Waco Clifford Linedecker (St. Martins Paperback, 1993)

Wicca

- The Law Enforcement Guide to Wicca Kerr Cuhulain (Horned Owl Publishing, 1997)

"Word of Faith" Movement

- Christianity in Crisis Hank Hanegraff (Harvest House Publishers, Inc, 1997)

- The Confusing World of Benny Hinn G. Richard Fisher and M. Kurt Goedelman (Personal Freedom Outreach, 1997)

- A Different Gospel - A Historical and Biblical Analysis of the Modern Faith Movement D. R. McConnell (Hendrickson Publishers Inc., 1988)

- The Walking Wounded-A Look at Faith Theology Jeremy Reynalds (Huntington House Publishers Lafayette, LA, 1996)

Worldwide Church of God

On Angels Wings: A Spiritual Journey Patricia Ann Laessig (Authorhouse)

Reference and Sources

Beyond The Da Vinci Code – René Chandelle

Combating Cult Mind Control – Steve Hassan

Cults: Prophecies, Practices and Personalities - Michael Jordan

Inside The Brotherhood: Further Secrets of the Freemasons – Martin Short

Leaving the Saints – Martha Beck

The Brotherhood - Stephen Knight

The Deceivers: What Cults Believe - Josh Mcdowell and Don Stewart

The Secret World of Cults - Sarah Moran

The Rough Guide to Conspiracy Theories – James McConnchie and Robin Tudge

Other Titles by Robin Jackson

Losing The Faith: Truth under Scrutiny

Robin Jackson has written a heart wrenching, yet inspiring account about his battle to come to terms with the conflicting teachings, deception, and cover-ups of the religious cult he became a member of at the tender age of 13.

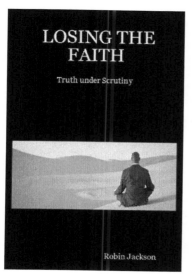

The story begins with the author transporting the reader back to his childhood days and early life influences. It chronicles Robin Jackson's subsequent journey through the cult he was led to believe is "God's sole collective channel for the flow of Biblical truth to men".

Jackson's story will take you through the highs and lows, joys and tragedies, and to the depths of despair, which eventually leads to his exit from the organization known as Jehovah's Witnesses. This book will inspire anyone who needs to get out of a destructive mind control cult.

Losing The Faith is a powerful and touching account of man's journey to freedom from repression and religious intolerance.

Losing The Faith – Truth under Scrutiny is available internationally at www.lulu.com/robinjackson

For South African distribution and information send email to jacko@mtnloaded.co.za